SUMMER HEAT

DAVID P. HOPE

Published by Rambling Star Publishing
Mechanicsville, VA
USA

To my parents, Philip H. Hope Jr. and Marvel A. Hope.

ACKNOWLEDGMENTS

This work is dedicated to my parents, Philip H. Hope Jr. and Marvel A. Hope, who individually and together strove daily to provide a safe home and a nurturing environment for their two children. They gave their best for the advancement of us. A Christian environment with an emphasis on service to others influenced both my sister and me. They instilled a strong sense of right and wrong. Further, one was to complete any task or challenge undertaken. We were given a strong base from which to build our lives.

I must say "thank you" and "love" to my big sister, Sylvia, such a wonderful person. While she must be kept busy praying for her adult children and their children, she prays for me too, which means more to me than words can express.

The men and women of the Chesterfield County Police Department hold a special place in my heart, a number of whom are mentioned in this writing. Some should be recognized by name, but others who daily or monthly impacted my career would be unfairly left un-named. Suffice it to say that my development as a police officer as I climbed up the chain of command was directly influenced by fellow officers, supervisors, management, and the chief himself. Thank you to all, for a wonderful career and an unmatched brother and sisterhood.

The crew of *Summer Heat* to a person cannot adequately be acknowledged for their tenacity, individual strengths, team work, sacrifice to the others, bravery, and love, all demonstrated time and again under the most dangerous, life threatening, and challenging of situations. Love, thanks, and the utmost respect to all: Dave Graf, Jeff Akins, Hannah Combs, and Jammer the Wonder Dog.

To Captain John Hess, Chief Mate Robin Espinosa, and the crew of then CSX *Discovery*, thank you for your bravery and for saving our lives. Extraordinary measures were taken to pluck the crew of *Summer Heat* from certain peril. Both the ship and her crew were certainly at risk throughout the rescue effort. The *Summer Heat* crew will never forget CSX *Discovery* and her very professional crew. Again, thank you.

Finally, I thank Camilla, my fiancée, for coming into my life and providing the love and support that she does through challenging times. And Camilla, thank you for helping me complete my dream of sailing to the islands!

TABLE OF CONTENTS

PREFACE

"TELL DAVE HE NEEDS TO COME BACK UP HERE!"

I heard these words being shouted out from my second mate and alternate watch captain, David "Dave" Graf. My cousin, Jeff Akins, slid open the companionway hatch to hail me, and I was already putting on my foul-weather gear, inflatable personal flotation device, and tether for the umpteenth time in the last four days. We were on board *Summer Heat*, my 37' Hunter 376 sloop-rigged sailboat, en route to the Bahamas from Beaufort, North Carolina, and the weather was giving us a beating.

As I struggled up the companionway ladder, with the boat pitching violently sideways as well as fore and aft, Dave instructed me to look at the radar. After clipping the tether in to the jack line to stay attached to the boat, I grabbed a handhold and swung my body behind the ship's wheel to see the radar.

"Look at that storm that is heading directly toward us!" Dave yelled.

"Yeah, it looks like Pac Man coming to get us," I replied. "I think we are in for it this time!"

I had finished my watch about two hours earlier and had been called back up on deck for a previous "Pac Man" encounter. That one had been benign enough, with only massive clouds and no more wind than the 35 to 40 knots we were already experiencing. Pac Man

Number Two looked much more threatening as it ate up the screen in approach of our position.

We caught glimpses of moon as heavy clouds passed under its glow. The moon had been reassuring earlier on as it led us to believe that the storm was breaking up. Now, the moon was a dastardly liar, making unfulfilled promises, luring us into a false sense of security.

Three of our five crew members were on deck while our first mate, Hannah Combs, was off watch, trying to rest down below with Jammer the wonder dog, who was trying to find a paw hold somewhere in the aft cabin. Dave, Jeff, and I sat lurching and trying our best to hold on while discussing our options and waiting for Pac Man Number Two to come and devour us. The moon disappeared, and the sky grew heavy with fast-moving storm clouds.

The wind increased dramatically – we learned later that the wind gusted to 50 knots that night. *Summer Heat* had been motor sailing with a double-reefed mainsail and no jib sail, trying to make some southing toward the Abacos. This put the wind almost directly on the bow. When a sudden, strong blast of wind hit *Summer Heat* from starboard, it caused her to heel instantly almost ninety degrees to port. I heard an "Oh no!" well up from somewhere within me and screech out into the cockpit, though I doubt that anyone else heard my plea through the crashing of boat against waves and the howling of the wind. Miraculously, *Summer Heat* regained her feet and did not sustain a full knock down. A bit shaken, but physically alright and regaining my composure, I asked myself, "How did I get here?"

CHAPTER 1
THE EARLY YEARS

A SERIES OF EVENTS contributed to the boat and crew being in harm's way that night and the following fateful day.

We hope that all of life's experiences, totaled up, will be enough to see us through the really difficult times, sometimes perhaps life-threatening times, such as the loss of a boat, a devastating accident, or a serious illness. All of life's experiences, not just the good ones, come into play when we are faced with challenges. Hopefully, we learn as much from our failures as our successes. When push comes to shove, we rely on all that we have learned over the years, from every aspect of our lives. This is how it all started.

My dad, Philip H. Hope Jr., was born and raised in St. Michaels on the Eastern Shore of Maryland. He met my mother in Miami Beach during WWII and they moved to St. Michaels shortly after the war. The closest hospital was nine miles away in Easton so that's where I was born.

My mother, father, sister, and I lived in St. Michaels, with a six-month stay back in Florida until I was three and a half years old, and then we moved to Virginia. Our family made annual trips to St. Michaels to visit Dad's family, and it was here that my love for the water began.

Dad always took me down to the waterfront, which was very much a working waterfront at the time, with Chesapeake deadrise boats and huge warehouses to accommodate the catches of crabs, oysters, and mano clams. We enjoyed looking at the various boats, mostly workboats, but also the few pleasure boats that were tied up at the docks.

On one visit, Dad's brother, Doug, borrowed a Chris-Craft–style runabout for the afternoon and the three of us went for a ride out through the little harbor of St. Michaels and on to the Miles River. One of my favorite memories is of passing other boats and the occupants waving to us. I was very young at the time, but I was smitten by that boat ride.

At the far end of Chestnut Street, a block from my grandparents' house, was "Back Creek," the proper name being San Domingo Creek. We spent many hours there just standing on the work dock, looking at the old deadrise workboats and beyond to the winding creek.

During one visit, Dad borrowed a friend's boat and took me down that creek. It was quite an adventure, just the two of us on a gloriously beautiful day, riding down Back Creek. We pulled up on a small beach and waded in the cool, salty water, which was a stretch for my dad as he could not swim a lick.

My mother made sure that I knew how to swim, though. When I was five years old my immediate family and my uncle's family on my mother's side spent a Sunday afternoon at Red Water Lake for a family picnic. Red Water Lake was a manmade swimming lake with boardwalks, diving platforms, and a sand beach. My cousin, Larry, a year older and about a head taller than me, and I were standing on the boardwalk that led out to the deep water, and Larry, being the brazen and adventurous type, said to me: "Look where I can jump!" He immediately walked a little farther out toward the deep end, jumped in and landed in waist-deep water. So I said: "Look where I can jump," went a little farther out and jumped into chest-high water.

Larry proved that he could go out a few more steps and jumped into shoulder-deep water. Not to be out done, I walked a little farther down the boardwalk: "Look where I can jump!"

Much to his credit, Larry yelled "Don't do it!" but in I went. I saw legs, arms, and bubbles floating up through the green water and beams of sunlight filtering down. That's all that I remember. Someone pulled me out and that was the end of "swimming" for the day.

Sometimes fate, luck, or God intervene into the events of life. I believe the latter of the three is responsible. Later, my mother forced me to take swimming lessons, which I greatly disliked, but, the lessons opened up a new world to me. That was followed by membership in the Boy Scouts of America, where advancement in rank required swimming and various accomplishments in swimming. I do not think that I would enjoy the water nearly as much as I do had it not been for the insistence of my mother that I learn to swim and the swimming requirements in Scouting at the time.

In Virginia, I was raised in the small industrial town of Hopewell. The Heckel family — mother, dad, and four children — lived across the street. We kids were all fast friends, and the adults were too. Dr. Heckel, a chemist with Allied Chemical Company, as it was called then, bought a thirty-something foot cabin cruiser and later upgraded to a forty-something footer. He graciously invited me on a number of trips with his family, which only further encouraged my love of boats.

The confluence of the James River and the Appomattox River is located at City Point, which is a part of Hopewell, thus providing numerous places to explore by water. I couldn't think of anything more fun than spending time on those boats.

Then an unlikely thing happened. Dr. Heckel sold the forty-something powerboat and bought an approximately eighteen-foot sailboat. That made absolutely no sense to me — until I went sailing on this new craft.

When we were teenagers, Carl and Harry Heckel III, Leroy Brogdon, and I sailed the eighteen-foot sailboat down the James River from Hopewell about 20 miles or so to a campground known as Sunken Meadows. As we approached Sunken Meadows a squall blew up with dark clouds and wind that quickly enveloped us. Carl and Harry were the only ones who knew how to sail the boat, and they scrambled to regain control. As the wind increased the boat heeled and her speed increased dramatically — we were flying! Now I was really hooked on sailing.

Several weeks later, in high school English class, we were charged with making a speech about any recent event or hobby in which we were involved. I reported on the sailing trip, and a fellow student talked about water skiing. There was a question-and-answer session after each presentation, and the water skier challenged me on my statement that sailing was exciting. During my high school years I was shy and generally had little to say, but somehow I rose to the challenge and quite effectively spoke to the excitement of sailing and, surprisingly, received high praise from the teacher.

Dr. Heckel, meanwhile, has recently finished his second solo circumnavigation of the world and at age 89 is the oldest man to have accomplished such a feat. He is still an inspiration to me although I have no interest in sailing around the world. Maybe I'll eat those words one day.

While Dad was born in a water town, Mother was born with wanderlust and a love of any good beach. I inherited her love for the beach and the smell of the ocean and learned to enjoy travel as I matured. The two of them, and all of these experiences, contributed to my love of sailing and cruising under sail.

CHAPTER 2
DON'T DO ANYTHING STUPID

THOUGHTS OF SAILING or any type of boating took a distant back seat as life progressed toward college, girls, and the possibility of going to war. After three years of floundering around in college, not knowing what I wanted to do with my life, it was crossroads time. I came home for the summer.

Not happy with my performance and lack of discipline at school, I decided to talk with the army recruiter. This was not a brilliant move on my part as this was 1968 and the war in Vietnam was raging. My mother saw me off to the recruiter's office with the admonition: "Don't do anything stupid, like signing up."

I assured her that I would not. I had spent two years in Air Force R.O.T.C. during the first two years of college and wanted to be a military officer, but this had not been incentive enough to study hard and stay in school.

The recruiter said that he could not guarantee that I would go to Officer Candidate School (O.C.S.) without a college degree, but my test scores were high enough that entry into O.C. S. should present no problem. I came home and told my mother that I had enlisted in the U.S. Army. I believe she thought that I had totally lost my mind.

Within two weeks, I was on a train to Fort Benning, Georgia, affectionately known as "Benning School for Boys." While basic training was no picnic in 1968, I saw it as a serious game that had to be played and had to be won. An upper-respiratory infection almost did me in, but I got out of the hospital just in time to remain with my basic training company and graduate on time.

I did go to O.C.S. at the Infantry School at Fort Benning, and graduated as a brand-new second lieutenant in September 1969. I managed to spend two very hot summers at Fort Benning, one for basic training and one for O.C.S.

Once again, God intervened in my stupidity. Everyone knew that the life expectancy of a second lieutenant in Vietnam was very short, the rumor being 18 seconds during action. About halfway through my stint in O.C.S., the army decided that it needed some signal corps officers, and my company had to supply eight volunteers. Never volunteer for anything in the army, right? Not in this case. I ran as fast as I could down those stairs to the commanding officer's office and signed on the dotted line.

In the back of my mind I wondered if this was a trick. Would I be up all night doing pushups and sit-ups for falling for such a stupid ploy? It wasn't a trick, but I was up most of the night completing paperwork for the possible branch transfer upon the assumed graduation. I really didn't believe that the transfer would happen so I put all of that exercise behind me and continued on with the daily training and harassment that was O.C.S. A few weeks went by and I learned that the army was looking for helicopter pilots. "Hey," I thought, "that has to be a lot safer than being an infantry lieutenant, right?"

I passed the written test with flying colors and was getting very excited about the idea of being a helicopter pilot. Then came the vision test. I passed the distance-vision test but failed the close-up test. I was heartbroken. Once again, however, it was divine intervention. During O.C.S. we didn't have much access to the current news, and I didn't understand the very serious hazards of flying a helicopter in Vietnam – they were getting shot down regularly.

The day before graduation, the company first sergeant read out the assignment orders for all of the graduating candidates. He read off 132 assignments and did not call my name. The first sergeant asked if there were any questions and I raised my hand, keeping in mind that there was still one more day until graduation and being released from the tortures of O.C.S.

"First Sergeant," I said. "You didn't read off my name."

He looked at me, then looked down at the clipboard in his hand and said: "Hope, you are going to the signal corps, Signal Officer Basic School, Fort Gordon, Georgia."

A wide grin rose on my face.

"Wipe that grin off your face, candidate, you still have one day to go!" the first sergeant snapped authoritatively.

"Yes, First Sergeant," I said meekly, celebrating wildly inside.

We graduated 133 students out of a class of 220. Generally, when a candidate dropped out or was washed out, he had thirty days of leave before going to Vietnam as an infantryman. This was with several exceptions. Sadly, two of our classmates who had been sent to Vietnam as enlisted men were killed before the rest of the class graduated from O.C.S.

In the spring of 1972 divine intervention struck again. I had six months to go until I could be released from active duty and I needed to make a decision about staying in or leaving the army. I liked life in the army as a junior officer but could not make a career of it without that college degree that I had frittered away. I was about to go on two weeks of annual leave and was in turmoil about this impending decision. "Why do today what you can put off until tomorrow," I thought. "Let's make that weighty decision after thinking about it during vacation."

But a little voice was nagging me: "Make up your mind now."

And for once, I listened. I picked up the telephone and called officer personnel at The Pentagon and requested that the army start the paperwork to end my voluntary indefinite status. This was to take approximately six months, and then I would be released from active duty.

Upon my return from two weeks of leave, I found an envelope waiting on my desk. Inside were orders sending me to the Republic of South Vietnam. I read it several times and then picked up the phone and again called officer personnel in The Pentagon. I explained to the voice on the other end of the line that I had just received orders to Vietnam, but explained that two weeks earlier I had called officer personnel requesting to end my active-duty status. The voice said: "Hold on, let me check this out."

What seemed like hours went by while I waited on hold, then the voice came back and said: "You are right, you are getting out of the army in September. Disregard the orders."

Wow. I had always expected to go to Vietnam at some point, and was obviously very glad and thankful to not actually go.

I did get some time on the water during my army days as my best friend from high school was back in the area. He was a naval officer stationed in Norfolk, Virginia, and we did some water skiing on his dad's 16' tri-hull runabout. Every weekend possible, we went water skiing at the "gravel pit" off of the James River near Richmond. After mastering slalom skiing, we tried climbing up the back of the skier and riding on his shoulders. That was a fairly difficult feat to pull off with a 65 horsepower outboard motor. We managed to do it a couple of times, but September came and it was time for me to go back to college.

CHAPTER 3
BACK TO COLLEGE AND CAMPUS POLICE

This time I was determined to succeed. I had worked in army television production for two years and thought I wanted to pursue this field as a career, but my part-time job at a local television station fell through and I needed employment. After bouncing around a bit, I took a job as a campus police officer. The director of security had been an army intelligence officer and liked that I had been a lieutenant. After working as a campus police officer for a short while, I discovered that I liked the idea of catching "bad guys" and putting them in jail. I changed my major to criminal justice and in three and a half more years, finished my degree.

Not a lot happened nightly while performing foot patrols as a campus police officer. Once in a while a foot pursuit would ensue over some criminal violation or another. Being in my mid-twenties, I was still pretty fast afoot and won the foot pursuits in which I was involved. Generally, some desperado got tackled and was then taken before the local magistrate to face a probable-cause hearing to be incarcerated for the evening. Usually, the shifts were long and boring, with little to do but walk around and stay alert. One evening, though, I encountered the first significant case of my law-enforcement career.

While patrolling the end of campus that encompassed the women's dorms, I was approached by a young man who said excitedly,

"Officer, there is a guy behind the dorm who is beating the hell out of a naked female student!"

I sprinted from the front of the dorm to the rear parking lot and sure enough found a white male with long, stringy hair and a much disheveled appearance standing over an unclothed college-aged white female. He was actively swinging away at her, striking blows against her head and body. He was so intent on what he was doing that he never realized that I was approaching.

I grabbed him from behind and quickly took him to the ground and handcuffed him before he could muster much resistance. I quickly determined that he was both drunk and high on drugs and was so impaired that most likely a baby could have cuffed him. He had enough left in him to have pounded on the young woman, however. I called for the patrol car for the suspect and a rescue vehicle for the badly assaulted female student.

I instructed a bystander to get a blanket to cover the victim's naked, bruised, and burned body. She had suffered two stove burns to her back. Her face was so swollen that two months later when the case went to court, I could not recognize her after her face had returned to its natural state.

I stood the suspect up and conducted a search incidental to arrest of his person. In his jacket I found two large drug bottles, one in each pocket. These were the dark brown bottles from which pharmacists dispense medications. They were not the small bottles that one gets with a prescription.

While waiting for the campus patrol car to arrive, I contacted a good friend who worked with the Greenville City police department as a narcotics detective and told him about the drugs I had found. Campus police and the city police shared the same radio frequency, and shortly two city narcotics officers were en route to my location.

During that time, the campus police car, being driven by the shift lieutenant, arrived on the scene. The suspect, who had been screaming his head off since my arrival, had not calmed down. The lieutenant exited the police car and approached me. I again stood up the suspect so that he could be placed in the patrol car. As the lieutenant got close, the suspect drew up a disgusting hock of spit and spit it directly in the lieutenant's face. It happened so quickly that there was not time to react to prevent the act or turn away from it. The lieutenant was an older man who certainly did not deserve that reaction to his presence. I really expected the lieutenant to respond physically, but, much to his credit, he restrained himself and simply took out a handkerchief and wiped the spit away. I didn't know the man very well at all, but I felt quite sorry for him that night.

When my two narcotics detective friends arrived and examined the drug bottles that I had recovered, they told me about a drugstore burglary that had taken place just a couple of nights prior in Robersonville, North Carolina, a few miles away. They said that a large number of barbiturates had been stolen from the store.

Upon returning to their office, the narcs quickly matched the bottles to the drugstore burglary. They obtained a search warrant, and we drove out to the trailer park listed as the suspect's address on his driver license. We had three jurisdictions of law enforcement officers with us – East Carolina University Campus Police, Greenville City Police, and deputies from the Pitt County Sheriff's Office. The trailer park was just outside Greenville city limits, thus, the need for the Pitt County Sheriff's deputies.

As we approached the trailer, we observed pills along the walkway leading to the trailer entrance. The front door was open, and we observed pills on the floor immediately inside the trailer. There were pills on the floor throughout the living room and pills on the couch. Empty beer cans and liquor bottles abounded throughout the room. A used tampon was resting on the end table beside the couch. We found two naked white males, in their twenties, passed out in bed together. They were placed under arrest and put in a patrol car.

I rode with that officer to take the prisoners before the magistrate. Whoever searched the prisoners before they were placed in the car was not thorough. As we drove down the dirt road from the trailer park to the highway, there was rummaging around from the back seat. Even though they were hand cuffed, the prisoners somehow retrieved pills from their pants pockets and were eating them. A lesson learned.

Later that night, it was learned that the naked girl and her assailant were girlfriend and boyfriend. Five or six young people had been at the trailer all weekend and were partying on the drugs that they had stolen from the Robersonville drugstore. The boyfriend had gotten out of bed and went with one of the other males to the store to get more beer. Upon his return, the boyfriend found that one of the other males had taken his place in bed with the girlfriend, thus, the severe beating. During the beating, the girl was forced against the gas stove and the boyfriend intentionally turned on the burner and burned the girl's back in two places. Apparently he was so disgusted with her that he forced her into the car and took her back to her dorm at ECU. Of course she was still naked and he had to beat her some more before he would be satisfied.

In court a couple of months later, the victim's attorney pleaded that the couple was now engaged to be married and that the victim wished for the assault charge to be dropped. Both sets of parents were present. The narcotics officers did get convictions for the drugs and the burglary, and those responsible went to prison for those offenses.

CHAPTER 4
A BRIEF ENCOUNTER WITH SAILING

MY NEXT ENCOUNTER with sailing happened a year or two later. Dad was a long-term Boy Scout Troop Master. He served more than 50 years during his lifetime. He and members of the troop committee were taking the troop to the annual week-long summer camp at Eagle Point on Kerr Lake, Virginia. Dad carried me as an assistant scout master on his scouting rolls and asked if I could join the group for the week and serve as water activities coordinator. That was a great job in itself, but it also served to get me out of supervising breakfast and lunch preparation and clean up. What a great deal.

Mid-week, the older brother of one of the scouts arrived in camp with a sailboat in tow. During the early afternoon lull in activity due to lunch clean up, the brother invited me to go for a sail. I might have dropped a hint that I liked sailboats. We spent an hour or so sailing in light wind, just off of Eagle Point.

After a bit he handed the tiller to me and said to just watch the wind and steer accordingly. Yes, he had described what the wind should look like as it came across the water but to no avail. I couldn't see that wind if my life depended on it. The sailing was good, not as exciting as being in the squall with the Heckel boys, but good. I was disappointed that I didn't have a clue as to how to actually sail the boat. See the wind, are you kidding me? The seed was still there, but it had to lie dormant for a while longer.

CHAPTER 5
A NEW LOCATION AND NEW CAREER

AFTER GRADUATING FROM EAST CAROLINA UNIVERSITY with a B.S.P. in Criminal Justice in August of 1976, I accepted a position as police officer with the Chesterfield County Police Department in, Chesterfield, Virginia. I had applied to several local agencies but felt that Chesterfield was a good fit for me and had the most to offer. I had considered several resort communities as a place of employment but ultimately decided to return closer to home. My parents lived at the far eastern end of the county and this would allow me to spend time with them. Besides, my lack of 20/20 vision prohibited me from pursuing most of the federal law enforcement jobs in which I would have been interested.

Local law enforcement is many things: exciting, boring, stressful, service oriented, full of long hours, angst ridden, a brother-sisterhood, rewarding (not financially), both fulfilling and not, fun, and a profession of which one can be proud. Oh, and did I mention dangerous?

The events that happened during my law-enforcement career led me toward active pursuits in my off-duty time. Most of these pursuits were water related and led ultimately to sailing once again. If you have some understanding of the stresses and dangers of street police work (supervision and management come with their own issues), you will understand the draw toward sailing, with its own stressors, excitement, and sometimes boredom but always fun. All of my water sports served to take me away from the stressors of the job, clear my head, and ready me to jump back in to the fray.

As my career advanced, so did my water-related recreational activities, with sailing being the pinnacle of those sports. I would like to share some of both, the police events and the progression to sailing and the learning curve of each.

I joined law enforcement for the usual reasons, to help others and to put the "bad guys" in jail. The police basic-training school was easy for me academically as I had just graduated college and was used to sitting in class and doing the requisite studying at night. My army basic training and officer candidate's school took care of the discipline and the regimented training offered at the police academy. Fire arms training required some concentration since we were using .38 revolvers at the time and not the military weaponry to which I was exposed in the U.S. Army. I have always liked shooting guns so it was not an issue. For a few police trainees it was an issue because they had never fired any type of weapon in their entire lives. If you cannot qualify on the firing range, you cannot be a police officer.

I never quite understood how someone thought he or she wanted to be a police officer but was uncomfortable shooting a weapon. For some, the firearms training was intimidating. It started benignly enough in the classroom, where we learned about sight picture, sight alignment, trigger squeeze, cleaning the firearm, weapon retention, shoot/don't shoot situations and other various topics. The pucker factor increased when the instructor talked about liability issues and the ramifications of actually shooting someone.

Most of us enjoyed our time on the firing range, keeping in mind that we really did need to qualify with our weapons. There was tension on the firing line. The range officers maintained strict control of the recruits to ensure that no one other than the paper targets got shot. Eight shooters would line up on the range at a time. The course of fire was explained by the range officer via a loud speaker. Sometimes instructions were a little difficult to understand while wearing ear muffs for protection from the loud report of the weapons.

The physical comfort level was never at neutral, nor should it have been. It was either too hot or too cold on the outdoor range. The sun was in our eyes, and the target was in the shade. The ear muffs didn't fit right. Our hands were sweaty and we were worried about the grip.

After the course of fire had been explained, the range officer would say what the immediate line of fire would be. Then he would blow the whistle, signifying to draw and fire. It went something like this: "Shooters, at the whistle, you will draw and fire your weapon two times in three seconds and holster your weapon. When un-holstered, always keep your weapon pointed down range. If you have any problem, keep your weapon pointing down range and raise your non-weapon hand. A range officer will come to you immediately. All ready on the right, all ready on the left, all ready on the firing line. Stand by."

Then, a blast of the whistle and you had three seconds to somehow get the revolver out of the holster, which was snapped in, point it down range at your own target and shoot two times, hopefully hitting the target center mass. Piece of cake.

What you did not want to hear was the range officer screaming your name through the PA speaker because of some stupid unsafe move that you just made. To set the record straight, firearms training has come a long way since then. Departments currently use pop up or flip silhouette targets that turn for a set time. Whistles are not used as the shooter must look for the target to present itself. Even back then, experienced officers utilized practical shooting exercises, such as tactically exiting a police vehicle and running for cover, then firing at the "assailant."

At the end of the hand-gun training, I was tied with one other recruit for first place in shooting scores. Nick had been shooting all of his life; I had been shooting hand guns only briefly. We had a "shoot off" to determine who would receive the first place plaque at the graduation ceremony, and I wanted that award.

While Nick and I were the only ones really in contention at that point, the entire class participated. I could see where my bullets were impacting the target and I was doing well. This was a timed course of fire at a silhouette target, draw and fire two times in three seconds. Do this three times. Draw and fire six shots in eight seconds. Draw and fire six shots, re-load and fire six more shots, all in maybe 20 seconds. Drop back to the 30 yard line and draw and fire 18 shots (total) in 45 seconds.

Somewhere on that last string of fire I lost concentration and I knew it. I shot in the upper nineties on the target, but it was not good enough. Nick had beaten me. There was nothing to do about it. I finished second in a class of 35 for the shooting award.

A sailboat racing friend of mine says there is only one winner, all others are losers. I understand the sentiment but don't subscribe to it, although I must say that only one person's name was read out at graduation and only one person went up on stage to receive the plaque from our chief of police and from the academy director.

On the day before the last day of class, the student test scores were read out to the class. Our shooting qualification score counted in the mix. I was at or near the top of the class. The final exam was to be the next day, the last day of the academy. We were all planning to go out that evening to celebrate the end of the academy and our graduation.

I thought if I were to stay in for a while and do a proper review, I just might get that Top Academic Achievement award. I had not pushed myself in college the first time around, and it cost me - and my parents too. For once I deferred gratification; I stayed in and did a complete review of all topics.

I did ultimately meet up with my friends for a couple of celebratory drinks. On my way down the hall to meet my friends, I saw a class mate, John, still pouring over the books. John was at the top of the academic heap too. I said to myself, "Study on, John," with that I went to meet my friends. This time, at the graduation ceremony, it was my name that was called and I was the one who shook the hand of my new chief of police as the plaque was handed to me by the academy director. My parents were there, and I was very glad that my mother could be proud of her son. John, by the way, finished second and for more than thirty years he has never let me forget that I beat him out. We are great friends to this day.

CHAPTER 6
A NEW WIFE AND A NEW SPORT

As MY POLICE CAREER began to take off, so did the rest of my adult life, all in preparation for the adventure of a lifetime. Within six months of employment with the Chesterfield County Police Department, I met my future wife. Six months after that, we were married. Teri and I had a great deal in common; in fact, one of my police buddies loved to say, "Look, Hope married his sister." We both had a love of the outdoors and particularly water sports.

While on our honeymoon in Nassau, Bahamas, in 1977, we saw a Bahamian attempting to sail what looked like a surfboard with a sail and mast attached to it. The sailor had to hold up the mast and sail with his own strength, and he was not meeting with a lot of success.

A couple of years later we were visiting the island of Bermuda with my parents and saw two of the same strange contraptions being sailed in a cove along the Bermuda coast. This couple was doing a little better than the Bahamian. By then, I understood that these things were windsurfers or sailboards.

The following summer, Teri and I were visiting Virginia Beach, Virginia, and while on the beach I saw two sailboards sail out into the Atlantic Ocean and around the fishing pier. "Wow, if they can do that, so can I!" I exclaimed with great enthusiasm.

Back in Chesterfield County, I had been transferred to the police personnel and training unit, where I was performing background investigations on prospective employees and permit applicants. One day around noon I was driving along the busy business district and saw a sailboard on display at a local motorcycle shop. The board was on the ground and the sail and mast were held aloft, being tied to a light post. I had to pull in to that shop. No choice. After asking a few questions, I knew I had to buy that board and rig.

The following Saturday, Teri and I jumped on my Honda 750 motorcycle and rode up to the motorcycle shop so that Teri could see the sailboard and, hopefully, give her blessing for me to make the purchase. When she saw the board up close, she was quickly convinced and suggested that we should see if we could find other boards from which to choose. We rode all over the greater Richmond area to every boat store that we could find, looking for sailboards. Surprisingly, several power boat marine sales stores had one or two boards on display. This was in the days of windsurfing infancy, and windsurfing shops had not yet been established on the East Coast. We opted for the first board that we had seen, a BIC Dufour Wing. Yes, BIC, of BIC pen fame. Price may have had some influence on our choice.

Before returning to the motorcycle shop to make the purchase, we decided to ride out to Swift Creek Reservoir in the hopes that someone might be out there wind-surfing so we could see how it goes. Sure enough, a fellow had just finished rigging his board when we pulled up beside a sandy spot on the road side adjacent to the water. The sail had a hair shampoo logo boldly emblazoned on it, so I assumed that the owner had won the board in some contest.

He floundered over and over again, trying to raise the sail out of the water and sail away. Each time, as the sail came out of the water, the sailor would fall over backward as the sail flew from the water to vertical, then over to the far side of the board. The momentum carried the sailor with the sail. Had I been thinking, I would have offered to buy that board and rig from him right then and there. Instead, we rode home, picked up the truck, and went to the motorcycle shop and bought the BIC board.

The very next day, Sunday, we went to the reservoir with our brand-new purchase and took turns learning to sail the board. I will never forget the complete elation that I felt the first time that I did not fall in the water while attempting to raise the sail. The board began to glide across the water with me standing on it and holding on to the wishbone boom, which was attached to the mast and held the rig in an upright position, catching the breeze. It dawned on me that I really had no clue as to how to turn around to get back to the starting point, but, then, I didn't care – I was sailing!

Time drew on and after a few trips to the reservoir, I was becoming pretty adventurous. At least twice, Teri had to drive the truck to the far side of the water to "rescue" me as the wind had increased and was overpowering me to the extent that I could not get back to our side of the reservoir. On one occasion, she rescued two of us, as an unknown fellow was in the same predicament as me. The whole process was exciting and I was really getting the sailing bug.

CHAPTER 7
EARLY CANOEING DAYS AND RISK

AT ABOUT THAT TIME, my canoeing days began. My cousin Larry owned an old aluminum Grumman canoe that had definitely seen better days. He and I took the boat out several times and then he encouraged me to take Teri. I have never liked borrowing things, but Larry insisted, and Teri and I enjoyed several nice trips in his Grumman. Our initial trips were very much trial and error.

Larry had introduced me to the joys of Swift Creek in Chesterfield County and Colonial Heights, Virginia. The creek was small and meandered through a rural part of Chesterfield before reaching Colonial Heights. Swift Creek was quite nice with over-hanging trees, wild flowers, rock gardens, and a wonderful remoteness. It was unlikely that we would meet another person while paddling that stretch of the creek.

The rapids were small, Class 1 and 2, with one solid Class 3 if the water was high. Sometimes in the summer, we would have to drag that "rock magnet," as aluminum canoes are called, over exposed rocks. Needless to say, aluminum canoes are not recommended for white-water canoeing.

After telling one of my police buddies, Mike, about the creek, he wanted to go. He borrowed a fiberglass canoe from another officer and met Teri and me at the put in location, where we unloaded the boats. We then took one truck to the take out location and returned to the put in to begin the trip.

We were adventurers, exploring the secrets of Swift Creek. Mike loaded up his canoe with a cooler and his police dog, Max, a large, aggressive German Shepherd. Teri and I also loaded a small cooler with fried chicken and a few beers. Our Chesapeake Bay Retriever, Commander, who weighed in at 90 lbs., accompanied us.

None of what we did that day is recommended, but at the time we did not know any better. It all most likely would have turned out just fine except that it had rained for a couple of days and the creek was swollen. Actually, at first, we were having an easy paddle of it, even with the additional water flow.

Commander loved the water and had canoed with us several times previously. He was an excellent swimmer and liked to swim along as we paddled. We always kept a close eye on him whenever he was allowed in the water.

The trip takes the better part of a day to complete. We were about three-quarters of the way through when we approached the only rapid on the creek that could be said to be challenging and only then when the water was high. The water was high, so Teri and I pulled our canoe to the side of the creek to scout the rapid. Teri and I had run this rapid several times before, but we always scouted it first as there was a certain route that led through the rocks and small boulders that made the rapid.

Mike also pulled his canoe to the side to see what we were up to, and when we told him that we were going to scout the rapid before running it, he seemed to think that was foolish and unnecessary. He was a little annoyed with us for being so cautious and jumped back into his canoe and took off downstream.

From our limited experience on Swift Creek, we knew that the beginning of the rapid should be run down the right side, then work toward the center, avoiding rocks and seeking out the clear path. Mike, not privy to that information, took off toward the center of the creek and was immediately swept toward the left center – not a good place to be.

Rather than finishing our scouting, we jumped into our canoe to stay close to Mike in case he needed help. This turned out to be a bad plan. The water really was running and to our inexperienced eyes, the rapid seemed huge, far larger than Teri and I had ever seen it.

Because we rushed into the situation rather than checking it out first, we were swept in the same general direction as Mike. He had gotten about 50 yards downstream of us in the worst part of the rapid when we saw his canoe fill up with water and turn over. The canoe, Mike, Max and the cooler went in four different directions, and all were being swept downstream quickly.

Max, not being a water dog, was swimming vertically, hind end straight down and the front paws paddling straight up and down, reaching for the sky. This was not very effective swimming, but he made it to shore. An additional problem was that this was early spring, March or April, and the water was cold. This was before any of us had wetsuits or even wool clothing. Blue jeans and heavy cotton shirts were the clothing of the day.

As we approached the same area, our boat began filling with water too. We were in big standing waves, which slowed us down and filled the boat. Our canoe was awash but upright. Commander thought that this would be an opportune time to go for a swim and jumped overboard. Teri and I had been doing a fairly good job of keeping the canoe upright until that instant. Commander pushed off to jump overboard, which was all it took to overturn the canoe. Things were bobbing everywhere as we were carried off downstream. Commander, of course, was having a grand old time. The humans were all gasping for air when the shock of the cold water hit us. We were at least wearing our personal floatation devices.

The rapid spit us out into a pool of calm water and we were able to gather up the canoes and a few belongings. All of the fried chicken went to the fish. I don't remember how, but we managed to start a campfire and warmed ourselves before continuing on. Mike lost his glasses when his canoe overturned and could see only blobs without them. The dogs were fine. It was a little chilly getting to the take out, but the campfire had elevated our core body heat and vigorous paddling helped maintain it as we headed for the end.

My cousin's canoe had a big dent in the bottom of it from being pinned against a rock. I hated to have to take it home to him. When he saw it, he laughed and later in the week, he and I took it to Larry's workplace, where Larry aluminum-welded it back together.

I did not borrow his canoe again.

CHAPTER 8
THE WHITE-WATER DAYS, DANGER ON THE RIVER

TERI AND I joined The Coastal Canoeists, a wonderful group of about six hundred folks who loved canoeing. The club was safety conscious, ecology minded, and focused on training. Trips were conducted every weekend of the year except for Christmas if it fell on a weekend. All trips were described via a newsletter so that the reader knew in advance what the degree of difficulty would be.

Safety rules had to be followed to help keep folks out of trouble. At least three canoes had to participate on each trip so that if someone overturned a canoe, the other two boats would be involved in the rescue. One boat would respond to the paddler and the second boat would gather up the flipped canoe and any other equipment that might be floating by. The swimmer's responsibility was to hold on to his/her paddle. Routinely, we collectively rescued each other, although I never considered these events to be rescues. We merely gathered up people and equipment and put them back together. Had we not been trained and possessed the proper equipment, the story would have been different and probably on the evening news.

For three years, we paddled every month of the year, wearing wetsuits and other protective gear in the winter. As we advanced in our skills, we switched to solo canoes and paddled the challenging streams of the Great Smoky Mountains. During our tandem days, we advanced beyond the yelling and who-is-in-charge syndrome to become a good tandem team. The solo boats were more maneuverable and their paddlers seemed to have more spontaneity or freedom to move quickly; thus, the decision to go solo was made.

Teri suffered two life-threatening experiences during our paddling years, neither of which was her fault.

Near the end of our tandem days, we were paddling the French Broad River in western North Carolina. The river had a strong flow that day and was stained brown with mud. We were about halfway through the day and had been handling some challenging conditions. With two people in the boat, she did not ride high in the bow as with a solo paddler. We had entered a long set of rapids with numerous standing waves. In fact, they were all around us. We were being rocketed thorough this section, but the canoe was quickly filling with water.

We had no time to bail; it was all we could do to keep the boat tracking forward. We knew not to turn sideways no matter what. Quickly the canoe became unresponsive due to the weight of the water and the waves slapping us around.

We knew the paddle strokes that one can employ to help stabilize a boat, but the event happened so quickly that we could not respond. The canoe turned over. Teri went one way, and I went the other.

Training says to stretch out flat and keep your feet downstream; even the club T-shirts said so. Keep your feet downstream. White water is generally shallow, and if a swimmer puts his feet down to try to stand up, there is a very strong chance that he will catch at least one foot between rocks.

While worrying about my own predicament, I was looking around for Teri. She was, for some reason, upstream of me and we were moving quickly farther apart, as I was being flushed downstream. Even though I was wearing a PFD, the raging water tried to push my head under water. I had to expend much effort to keep my head above water in the pushy conditions. We had a number of canoes and kayaks on the water that day and I was gathered up and reunited with our boat. I was farther downstream and Teri was still upstream, being rescued by a kayaker.

When we got back together in the canoe, Teri said that her lower torso had been caught against a rock and the water pressure prevented her from escaping. That was all she said about the subject.

Later, the kayaker, a member of our group, said to me, "Do you know that your wife almost bought the farm today?"

As he paddled toward her, he said, the water was pushing her head under water and she was fighting to get precious air. He lost sight of her a couple of times before reaching her. Ultimately, he paddled the bow of his kayak right up to her and she grabbed the rope loop that was attached to the bow. He paddled backward as hard as he could and with the help of the water flow, Teri was pulled off of that under-pinned rock. This was not a foot wedge, and the same thing would have happened to any one unlucky enough to be at that location. Teri seemed to shrug off the event and continued to paddle. She had always been more adventurous on our paddling trips than I had been.

By the following year we had switched to solo boats and were on the Smoky Mountain trip again. The solo boats were fun and certainly easier to handle. The Ocoee River in Georgia is dam controlled with cold strong water. A professional white-water raft had been supplied by a club member for any group of us who wanted to use it. Teri and I had already decided to raft the Ocoee rather than canoe it as our skills in the solo boats were good but not great. Friends talked us into using the free professional raft with no guide – note, no guide – rather than pay for a guided raft. I was against this from the start, but got out-voted.

Rafts must be guided and controlled rather than just floating down the river. None of the eight of us in that raft that day had any experience in a raft and certainly not on a challenging river like the Ocoee.

The very first rapid stopped us dead in our tracks, partially ejecting one of our party, who was pulled back in the raft by his pants belt. Quickly we moved to river's edge to bail as the raft had filled with water and became very unmanageable with the weight of the water sloshing around. One of the professionally guided rafts had problems there as well.

We continued down river, and we seemed to get a little control of the wild beast. Things were looking better until we had to face the double rapids of Buzz Saw and Diamond Splitter. Come on, Buzz Saw and Diamond Splitter? They're kidding right? Wrong. At about halfway through these two monsters I was catapulted into the air and landed on my hands and knees in the floor of the raft. As I regained control of my body I looked around and noticed that the three women who had been sitting on the port of the raft were no longer there.

The first young woman popped up from under the water and I grabbed her by the front of her PFD and struggled to pull her back into the raft. We were being swept through the rapid, heading to what disaster was next. She was hanging on to her paddle as she had been told to do, but the paddle was wedged between her and the raft, making it impossible to bend her torso into the raft. Some amount of time passed by during this encounter, seconds, a minute, I don't know.

Suddenly Teri popped up from under the raft, very much making animal sounds as she gasped for air. Now I was hanging on to two women by the fronts of their PFDs. All three women somehow got back in the boat and with the help of several of our kayakers, we got the raft under control and over to river's edge to re-group.

Teri was visibly shaken, as well she should have been. She later told me that she had been stuck under the raft and could not get away as her PFD floated her body up against the raft bottom. She said that finally she gave up, expecting to die. When she relaxed, the raft let her go and she popped up like a cork.

We sat on the side of the river, gathering our composure to finish the trip in the unguided raft. We had at least one more difficult rapid to encounter, "Hell Hole." Teri was still shaking and cold and uttered demonstratively, "I'm walking off this damn river."

I looked around at the steep cliffs that were immediately behind us and I looked up and down the river for a possible trail, to no avail. I put my arm around Teri and said, "Now Teri, it will be all right, we have to paddle off the river."

But I wasn't sure that I believed that it would really be all right. With much apprehension we climbed into the raft and once again started down river to face whatever would come next. "Hell Hole" was a large, raft-eating rapid that had to be skirted to our left as we passed. The trouble was that we had not been able to effectively steer/control the raft all day. What made us think that we could get by this new monster? The crew was extremely dedicated to being successful this time around, and after passing the rapid to port, we all erupted in celebration. The following half-mile to the take out was a flat-water piece of cake.

Shortly after that trip, I was promoted to sergeant and went back to street police work with only a few weekends off throughout the year. When we did paddle, Teri was not enthusiastic and often found reasons not to participate. She had hurt her wrist on a rock on a subsequent paddling trip, which turned out to be the last straw. When I asked why she didn't seem to be interested in canoeing any more, she reminded me of her two life-threatening events and said that it just wasn't fun anymore. No kidding. I think the first event would have done it for me.

I began devoting more time to windsurfing as it was something I could do alone and I was enjoying the challenge of sailing a board. Much of my vacation time was spent at the Outer Banks of North Carolina, learning how to sail in stronger winds and how to start in deep water. After learning to sail in 15 to 20 knots of wind, I was truly hooked on windsurfing and never looked back to my canoeing days again.

CHAPTER 9
DANGER ON THE STREETS

DANGER EXISTED FOR ME not only in my sports endeavors, but also in my profession. Danger comes for a number of reasons such as inexperience, relaxing too soon in any given situation, mental or physical exhaustion, heated encounters, overwhelming odds, desperate people, the fact that someone just wants to hurt you, and many more. Some encounters in hindsight seem so clearly foolish or lacking in good judgment, but that was not readily apparent at the time of the incident. Whatever the case, it was significantly important to understand what went well and what could have been done better.

I share a few life-threatening encounters throughout this writing, chronologically paralleling life in general. I believe that these encounters are linked to my desire to sail and played a role in our survival in the later sailing disaster.

From the time that I first began attending professional meetings as a young lieutenant and throughout my supervisory and management years with the police department, I carried a photograph of my first sailboat in my brief case. When meetings got tough or uncomfortable, I would sneak a look at the photograph and say, "One day..." It really did help.

Chesterfield Police officers patrol solo, but "back" fellow officer/s on potentially dangerous situations. On traffic stops, particularly at night, it is reassuring to see a fellow officer's police vehicle pulled up behind your own or sitting discretely across the street while you conduct your business. I had been with the department for a short while when one night on evening shift I was dispatched as a back-up officer to a residence in reference to a domestic dispute involving a man with a gun.

It is generally known that a domestic situation is the most dangerous call to which police officers must respond. Tempers run high, the officers are invading a man's "castle," it is embarrassing for the residents as the whole neighborhood knows that the police have been called, and all homes have weapons all over the house. Almost any object can be used as a weapon; it doesn't have to be a firearm, but firearms are the most dangerous, of course. Baseball bats, golf clubs, kitchen utensils, and lamp bases are a few of the objects that can readily be used to harm someone.

As I responded to this situation, I thought about what I might encounter and what my plan should be. Any plan will change upon arrival at the scene, but it is essential to have some idea of what you should do once on location.

Upon my arrival, I found the front yard to have several large trees in it. Two police cars were already on the scene. One officer was standing behind a tree, facing the house. I found a good thick tree and did the same. About that time, the man of the house stepped out of the front door and moved a short distance into the front yard. The officer who was assigned the call approached the man and asked about the problem there at the residence that evening.

I stepped from behind my position of relative safety and approached the officer and subject. The man was very agitated about an argument that had ensued inside the home with his wife. The investigating officer did a good job of calming the man, and I began to relax a little. At that point, the three of us were standing close together. The investigating officer said that there had been a report of a gun being involved in the incident and asked if the man did in fact have a gun. With that, and before the blink of an eye, the man quickly reached under his shirt and pulled a handgun out from the waist band of his pants and said, "Yes, here it is," as he handed it to the officer.

I don't know what the other officer thought, but I knew that the only thing that stopped one or both of us from being shot that night was that the man didn't want to shoot a police officer. Yes, he probably would have been killed, but so would at least one Chesterfield County Police Officer.

I thought about that event for a long time to come. The gun came out of the waist band so quickly that there was no time to react. Should we have stayed behind the trees and challenged the subject from there? If so, would he have run back into the house, possibly creating a hostage situation? Police work is inherently dangerous and police officers are expected to positively act. They are not, however, expected to blindly walk into the face of danger. That night, the gun was intended to impress someone inside the residence, not the police.

Weapons are often mentioned when an officer is dispatched to any given situation. While an officer should be on heightened alert, he or she may not be in an extreme officer safety mode. A fine line exists between complacency and being overly cautious. For example, it would be unacceptable for an officer to have his hand on his holstered handgun every time he approached a citizen. In some situations, it would be appropriate to have the weapon out.

CHAPTER 10
IT'S A SET UP, BEWARE

APPROXIMATELY A YEAR LATER, while working the day shift, two of us were dispatched to a police officer's residence. This officer was with a large adjoining police department but resided in Chesterfield County. Sensitive calls such as this one were dispatched via telephone rather than on the police radio, avoiding the police scanners that were prevalent at the time. The officer would be called on the radio to go to a telephone and call headquarters. That meant, call dispatch. That alone, caused the stress level to increase, knowing that something unusual was in the works.

We learned that this officer was home alone and was threatening suicide and had done so in the past. He was said to be unstable. He was known to our police dispatchers. This was another reason for the stress to increase.

Officer Alan Thompson and I responded to the residence. Neither of us had been to that location before and it took a few minutes to find the address. The neighborhood was near the county line and was an old neighborhood that was already depressed. The residence fit right in with the rest of the neighborhood. It could have used some spit and polish. We approached the house, knowing that this could prove to be a difficult encounter. A police officer who is the problem, not the solution, could create a challenging situation. He knows police procedure and what the police can and cannot do. He knows the law, understands his rights, and knows just how far he can push the envelope before crossing the line. Oh, and he has at least one firearm in the house and probably more.

After parking our police cars, Alan and I approached the residence on foot. Stepping onto the front porch, we saw that the front door was open with only the screen door being closed. We knocked on the wooden part of the screen door. No response. We knocked again and announced our presence. This time we heard a voice from back inside the house somewhere. The subject said to come in.

"No, you come to the door," we said.

"I can't, I'm in bed with no clothes on, come on in and come down the hall to the bedroom," he called back.

Talk about feeling as though we were being set up. We looked at each other, shrugged, and stepped inside the house with trepidation. We were young and still inexperienced police officers. I knew that we were being manipulated and I think Alan did too.

We slowly walked down the hall toward the bedroom, looking into side rooms as we passed.

"I'm back here in the bedroom, come on in," the voice said.

As we neared the "master" bedroom, we could begin to see inside and we saw that there was, in fact, someone lying prone in the bed and under the sheet. It was the police officer from the adjoining jurisdiction who had called in, threatening to kill himself.

Alan worked his way to the foot of the bed and I stood at right angle to the head of the bed. We talked for some time with the subject, listening as he described the tragedy of his messed-up life. While Alan and I were there to deal with a potentially suicidal subject, the interview began to take the tone of three officers discussing a rotten situation in which one of us found himself. Alan and I did not forget why we were there, but we did know that we were talking with a brother police officer.

Ultimately, the subject assured us that we had "talked him down," de-escalated the situation, that he no longer wanted to hurt himself, and that we could leave. He had calmed down dramatically and seemed to be tired and ready to rest. He had been lying on his back with both hands behind his head with his fingers interlaced, propping up his head while he talked. He said he had been up all night, unable to sleep.

He yawned and nonchalantly slid his hands under the sheet, reaching down toward his crotch as though to scratch himself.

"I guess I won't be needing this," he said, and lightning fast out came a police service revolver from under the sheet. Alan had a look of total disbelief on his face as he was still standing at the foot of the bed where the obvious first shot would be placed if it were to follow. It did not.

If the subject had wanted to, he could have shot Alan through the torso. I don't know if I could have wheeled around and gotten out of the room before he would have turned the gun on me or not. I would not have had time to draw and fire while standing there.

Alan and I never spoke of that encounter to each other. I was very ashamed of my performance that day and spoke of it to no one for years. Finally, I did begin telling other officers in the hope that they would learn from our mistakes.

CHAPTER 11
THE SHOT GUN AND THE DTS

LATE ONE NIGHT on the midnight shift, sometime around 3 AM, the police radio announced that a man was standing on his front porch firing a shotgun indiscriminately. Officer Jim Bourque was assigned the call, and Alan Thompson and I responded as back-up officers.

As I pulled up near the location, Alan was pulling in from the opposite direction, and Jim was already on location, crouched behind his patrol car. The suspect was, in fact, standing on his front porch with his shotgun in hand, in an offensive position. We, of course had our weapons out, each hiding behind a tree or a car.

Jim challenged the suspect verbally and within a few minutes the suspect placed his shotgun down on the deck of the porch. Jim had the suspect step out into the yard, away from the shotgun and we approached him with due caution.

When asked if he had been shooting the shotgun, the suspect said that he had been shooting at "them" because they had tried to enter his body. That was a rather strange thing to say, and we quickly realized that our man was not operating with a 'full deck' as the saying goes.

We entered the residence and began interviewing the suspect in earnest. As the interview progressed, we learned that the suspect was a full-blown alcoholic who was suffering through the D.T.s. His wife had left him several days ago, and since then he drank all the liquor in the house. That became readily evident as we saw numerous empty vodka bottles on the kitchen sink counter top.

"So tell us exactly what happened tonight," Jim said.

"I had lain down on the couch and fell asleep," the suspect said. "Something woke me up and I felt a heavy force on top of my body and I saw that 'he' was trying to enter my body by melding into me!"

The look on the suspect's face was one of stark terror. He said that this was not the first time that he had seen the red men with green eyes who tried to invade his body. Without a doubt, the suspect believed his hallucinations to be real. He had gone out on to the porch to shoot the red man who had been trying to meld into his body. Thus the justification for shooting up the neighborhood at 3AM.

We learned that a neighbor across the street was familiar with the suspect's condition and Jim went over there to investigate further, leaving Alan and me to deal with the hallucinating shot gunner. The suspect insisted on moving to the master bedroom to get some clothes, and Alan and I escorted him to that location. While there, the suspect began talking more about the red men who try to invade his body.

We attempted to steer the conversation in another direction, but the suspect was still reeling with the immediate and intense fear of the encounter on the couch. He again began to describe the red men. As he talked he got more excited and said, "Look, there is one of them now!" and pointed toward the corner of the room and asked, "Can't you see him?"

He uttered this with such sincerity that it was obvious that he thought the red man was standing right there. The suspect's eyebrows were up, and his eyes were wide open, and he began to tremble. If I didn't know better, I would have thought the red man was really there. I looked over at Alan and he was backed against the wall with a look on his face that said, "Let's get the heck out of here!"

We were still buying time with the suspect, waiting to see what Jim had learned from the neighbor across the street. Jim finally returned and said that while at the neighbor's house, he had been on the phone with the suspect's doctor. The doctor said that the suspect was suffering from D.T.s and needed to be hospitalized immediately. The doctor would contact the magistrate for the issuance of a mental warrant.

We immediately called for emergency medical transportation, which at that time consisted of a volunteer rescue squad. The suspect was finally calming down and when the emergency crew arrived, the suspect thanked us for intervening with the red men. Two days later, after being released from the hospital, the suspect made a formal complaint against all three of us for forcing him to go to the hospital. Sometimes doing the right thing just isn't enough, you just can't win. Oh well, no one got hurt that night.

CHAPTER 12
SMOKING IN THE BOYS' ROOM

DURING THIS SAME TIME FRAME I was transferred to the police personnel and training unit, where I primarily performed background investigations for the police department. The following story does not illustrate a particularly dangerous situation; although any law enforcement encounter can be dangerous; rather, it was the arrogance and stupidity of those who were involved that I wanted to share.

I had been assigned to the unit for approximately two days when this occurred. This was a suit or coat-and-tie assignment to conduct back-ground investigations, and my title was "investigator." Sometime during the day, I left the office to conduct an interview. My unmarked police car was parked in the outer parking lot, which was a good walk away from headquarters and carried one past the county jail.

While walking past the jail and by a number of parked cars, I noticed a strong odor of marijuana. It was pretty strange, smelling marijuana in the county government parking lot, to the side of the county jail and adjacent to the police department. I slowed my pace and looked around and, yes, I could definitely smell marijuana. Then I saw them, two heads slouched down in the front seat of a nondescript car parked directly outside the jail. I walked up the to the driver's-side window, which was rolled down, and witnessed the driver take a drag off a joint. He was very surprised to see me and when he did, he jammed the joint down between his legs and into his crotch. I guess I should have waited to see what was going to get hot first, but I reached in and pulled his hand from his crotch and he was still, unfortunately for him, holding on to the joint. What a place to smoke a joint. They were "toking up" before going to the jail to visit a friend. Now they were not only going to visit, but, they would get to stay for a while.

My new boss, the lieutenant in charge of personnel and training, thought that it was pretty cool that his new charge had made a drug arrest in the parking lot right outside of the office.

The only incident that I can think of that was more stupid than that was the time that some desperado decided to rob the bank that was a quarter-mile from police headquarters, at lunch time. Every police officer who worked in headquarters was headed out to lunch or getting ready to go to lunch when that event took place. As soon as the alarm was sounded, the bank and the highway were swarming with police officers, from the chief of police and members of his staff, to all types of detectives, to patrol officers who were close by. Police Captain Buck Maddra ran from his office to his police car, and was one of several officers who caught this brilliant bank robber.

CHAPTER 13
SPREADING MY SAILING WINGS

OFF DUTY, I was now attempting to hone my windsurfing skills. Warm weather days were spent at Swift Creek Reservoir, windsurfing in the fluky winds that abound in such an area. Directly across from the access point on the road side was the Greater Richmond Area Sailing Association. That organization possessed a long-term lease on a prime corner of the reservoir and turned it into a boat club. At that time, there were three small boat ramps, picnic tables, and a covered cooking area. I sailed over there one day and one of the members graciously invited me to join the club. I procrastinated and that cost me an extra year of waiting before we finally got our membership.

All of the boats were small, 18-foot being the largest boat in the club. After sailing on a member's beach catamaran, we knew that we had to have a cat.

Our first cat was a well-used Gulf Coast Cat, which was made to sail the Gulf Coast of Florida. This particular boat did well staying afloat in the parking lot. The hulls had been stressed where the cross member entered each hull. Of course, I was totally unaware of that problem; she looked like a great boat to me. She did prove to be fast, just don't turn her over. Beach cats are the best fun when they are just about to flip. Do you see a problem here?

We were able to sail the boat on the fringe season in cool weather, as we had wet suits from the canoeing days. Cats really are great fun. It takes little wind to get one moving, and a good puff will make her take off like a rocket ship. As the wind hits the sails, the fully battened mainsail will make a "pop" sound as it fills and takes the pressure of the wind. Next up is the acceleration and the rushing sound of the water as it passes by under the two hulls. The stronger the wind, the more the cat will heel to leeward (downwind) and at a critical balancing point, the windward (up wind) hull begins to lift out of the water. The most exciting time is trying to balance the cat on one hull without turning the boat over. That is not the fastest point of sail, as the leeward hull is digging into the water farther than the effective design of the hull, but it is great fun.

One spring Sunday afternoon, one of the club's hot-shot racing sailors wanted to take a spin on the G-Cat with me. We sailed out into the middle of the reservoir and I handed the tiller to Jim. This was a windy day, and Jim powered her up with the boat screaming across the water, eating up the distance as we flew. Suddenly, we heard a loud snap and the boat lost steerage.

Looking around, we discovered that the leeward rudder had snapped off at the water line. Fortunately, a cat has two rudders, one for each hull. We were over a mile away from the sailing club and decided we should start back. When we tacked, the existing rudder was then on the leeward side and, therefore, we had steerage. Jim, being the hot shot that he was, fired her up again and we took off. What a blast!

A good puff came along and Jim sheeted in the mainsail. The boat began to lift. The windward hull came out of the water and we were "flying a hull." Great stuff, but unfortunately, Jim's hull-flying technique wasn't the greatest, and the boat continued to lift to the point that she kept on going over on one side. Did I mention that this was the spring of the year? That water was cold!

To right a catamaran, the crew must stand on the bottom hull, the hull that is floating on the water with the other hull about seven feet in the air. Hopefully the boat has a "righting line" attached to both hulls so that the crew can grip the line, lean back and pull the mast, sails, and hull out of the water. It helps greatly if the mast is pointed into the wind so that as the mast lifts, the wind will catch under the sails and lift the boat. It also helps to have un-cleated the sails to prevent the boat from sailing away unattended as she is righted. Then there is the scramble for the crew to get back on board.

We got the boat righted, but as she came upright, another puff hit the main and the boat continued over onto her other side.

Now we heard a strange bubbling sound, like air escaping, quickly escaping. The stressed points on the bottom hull where the cross members connect were filling with water.

We had to stand on that hull in order to reach the top hull and the righting line. As the lower hull filled, the boat became unwieldy, and there was no balancing on that sinking hull. The boat sank to the top hull, which now was just floating on the water's surface. I was wearing a wet suit and got in the water to gather up the sails and tie them so that they would not be a hindrance. By the time that task was completed, I had no sense of feeling in my hands.

Power boats in general are not allowed on the reservoir, except for one small john boat, which happened to be on the water that day. Shortly, the john boat arrived and towed us slowly back to the boat club. In shallow water we righted the boat and got her on her trailer. One of the club members, who lived close by, rushed home and made hot tea and brought it back to us. That was the best hot tea that I have ever tasted.

Shortly after that encounter, the local Hobie cat dealer had a fantastic year-end sale, and Teri and I bought a reliable boat.

During the same time frame, a good friend invited us to go with him on a "barefoot" schooner cruise in the Bahamas. We flew to Nassau and boarded the schooner, *Fantome*, for a week of sailing the crystal-clear waters of the Bahamas. The *Fantome* carried 32 crew and 125 paying passengers. Sadly, a few years later the *Fantome* was lost at sea with several crew on board, as they tried valiantly to save her from a hurricane.

But we got to enjoy her in her glory days. As the ship left her dock in Nassau, a recording of the song "Amazing Grace," the bagpipe version, was played over the ship's public-address system. All hands, both crew and paying guests, were on deck. The mood was both exciting and romantic, and we headed out to sea. A couple of large cruise liners were in port, and those folks lined the rails of their ships to see us off. It was obvious that some of them clearly wanted to be on the *Fantome* with us. What looked like great fun turned out to be just that – great fun.

Fantome sailed all afternoon and through the night. The following morning we were anchored off of our first island, which we were eager to explore. *Fantome* was a deep-draft boat, and we had to board the launch to go to shore. The *Fantome* used two launches, and they ran every half hour to and from the island beach. Each evening and through the night, *Fantome* sailed to another destination, and each morning we would get in the launch, anticipating the day's activities, with snorkeling being at the top of the list. The snorkeling turned out to be the best I have ever seen. We were exposed to vibrantly colored tropical fish, many different types and colors of live coral, and once in a while, a small non-threatening shark.

By the trip's end, Teri and I were both hooked. We wanted a sailboat. Upon returning home, we investigated the sailboat possibilities and locations to keep such a boat. Driving all over southeastern Virginia, we discovered the small water town of Deltaville. Numerous marinas chock full of sailboats are located in Deltaville, and that location seemed to be the closest to our home in Chesterfield County, just south of Richmond. The drive one way was one and three-quarter hours, and we both decided that we were not yet ready to make that drive every time we wanted to go sailing.

We knew that we had to have some kind of boat to supplement the Hobie Cat. As it turned out, the same motorcycle shop that carried the sailboards now had a really hot-looking runabout power boat. I showed it to Teri, and we decided that a power boat would work for us for a few years. We toured all of the local marine shops and found a 19' Cobia cuddy cabin that fit the bill.

While I thoroughly enjoyed that boat, I discovered that after running her down the river for 15 minutes, I was ready to power down for some peace and quiet. The question became, what do I do now, after 15 minutes of burning gas just to run down the river? We both still enjoyed the boat but knew there had to be something more to come. That something came sooner than I expected.

CHAPTER 14
THE FIRST CRUISING SAILBOAT

FOR SEVERAL YEARS Teri and I had been going to the Virginia Beach Boat Show each February, mainly just for a weekend getaway in the winter. In the early 1990s, the Virginia Beach Boat Show exhibited a few sailboats along with the numerous and varied power boats that dominated the show. We climbed on the sailboats and did our share of drooling. As we walked out to the parking lot to leave one of the shows, Teri declared, "I want a sailboat." I replied, "I know you do, honey." She retorted, "No, you don't understand, I want a sailboat now!"

That started the search and ultimately led me down the road to *Summer Heat*.

The very next day, a Sunday, we were in Norfolk, Virginia, perusing the various marinas for boats. We had left the hotel in Virginia Beach and headed to Norfolk right after breakfast. The boats that we looked at that day were all too something – too old, too dilapidated, or too expensive. One boat that I liked the looks of turned out to have a spongy deck, as was pointed out by the next-door slip holder, who also pointed out that the owner's wife had "jumped ship," a term that would sometime later have more significance to me.

By the middle of March 1992 we found ourselves back in Deltaville looking at sailboats. As dusk was approaching, we drove up to the last marine sales business of the day. In fact, the lady was locking the front door of the business as I approached. She asked if she could help us, and I said that we were in the sailboat buying market, but I could see that she was closing for the day. She wanted to know the size and price range of our prospective boat. She said that she had a couple of boats that she would be glad to show us right then, and with that we drove a mile over to Sting Ray Harbor to see the candidates.

The second boat was an S2 9.2 center cockpit sailboat. The minute I stepped below on that boat, I knew it was the one.

Before the broker came down the companionway, I took Teri by the shoulders and whispered "This is the one!" She immediately agreed.

We drove the one and three-quarter hours back home to Chesterfield that night to think about it. But there was nothing to think about, other than "Are we crazy to even consider this?"

The following morning, after a relatively sleepless night, we were up early to drive back down to Deltaville to put a contract on "our" boat. It was a long ride to Deltaville, as I just knew someone else would snap up that wonderful boat before we could get there.

Carolyn, the owner of Norton's Yacht Sales, was glad to see us, and we were soon on the way to buying a real, monohull sailboat. One that we could sail to destinations, have meals on, and sleep on. Wow. The county credit union was excited to handle the loan, the largest for a boat to that date. The staff was unfamiliar with ship's documentation and other involved paperwork and thusly, were making demands of me that were about to make it difficult to consummate the loan. On the day before the loan was to be signed in Deltaville, the credit union staff was still being difficult. It looked to me as though the closing would not happen on the next day, Saturday.

In desperation, I picked up the telephone and called Carolyn and told her what was happening.

"Carolyn," I said, "buying a boat is supposed to be fun, and this is not fun."

She agreed and asked for the credit union staff's phone number. Within about 10 minutes, the staff member called me to say, meekly, that all had been worked out and the closing would go off without a hitch the following day, in Deltaville.

Unbeknownst to me, a whole new lifestyle had just begun. We named the boat *Razzle Dazzle*, in honor of Teri's nickname.

CHAPTER 15
PROMOTION TO SERGEANT AND A SERIOUS TEST

IN THE MEANTIME, life was changing for me at work as well. I had always said that if I could just get promoted to the rank of sergeant, I would be able to demonstrate my leadership skills and would move up in the organization, my ultimate goal. But I had to get that first promotion to make it onto the first rung of the promotional ladder.

With seven years of experience with the Chesterfield Police Department, I was promoted to the rank of sergeant. The Chief of Police, Colonel Joseph E. Pittman Jr., called me into his office and told me that he was promoting me to sergeant and said "Don't let me down."

The last thing anyone would ever want to do would be to let Joe Pittman down. I assured him in all earnestness that I would not let him down. I was elated. Finally, I was on the road to great things.

The promotion process was a daunting experience, with an exhaustive written exam, interviews, and evaluations from supervisors and managers. Exam questions came from a reading list of leadership texts, the police basic handbook, and, of course, the Code of Virginia. Some of the books were not readily accessible and required some effort to obtain. I had been through this process twice before and was very glad to have been selected.

After spending a year and a half supervising and conducting crime-prevention meetings and public-speaking engagements on behalf of the department, I was transferred to uniform operations, where I served as street supervisor on the evening shift, the busiest of the three shifts and where one is "baptized by fire."

Before my first tour of duty, I chose to ride with a fellow sergeant for an evening, on my own time, to acquaint myself with what was to follow. Sergeant Andy Scruggs who later retired as a deputy chief of police, and was a police basic classmate and friend, drove me all around the northern half of the county, showing me the hot spots with which I would have to deal.

At one point, we drove far out into one of the rural areas of the county where Andy showed me an old plantation house that had fallen on hard times. The house still had a "caretaker" and I use this term loosely, living on the property. The caretaker, Jim Sturm, was said to be a Vietnam veteran suffering from delayed stress syndrome.

As far as I could discern, later, Jim never served a day in the U.S. military. That proved to be the case with many misfits that we encountered over the years.

The plantation sat about 100 yards down a dirt drive, which was lined with mature oak trees, junk cars and pickup trucks, and discarded refrigerators and kitchen stoves. The approach to the residence was clearly dangerous, with many hiding places or points of possible ambush. Andy said that the department had received numerous calls for service at the residence and that if I ever had to go out there I should take plenty of people with me. I took his words seriously. Andy was a take charge sergeant, who knew his business.

Two weeks to a month later and no more, the inevitable happened. At approximately 9 PM, or 2100, one evening, I heard officer John Atkisson transmit across the police radio that he was in vehicular pursuit. The anxiety and excitement were evident in his transmissions. He was on a side road off of state Route 60, in the same rural area as that of Jim Sturm's residence, the old plantation.

At first, there was nothing to connect the two, but a pursuit is very serious in itself. I listened intently and started heading in the direction of the pursuit. The officer had been following the suspect pickup truck, when it suddenly veered off the rural road and out into a field where it ran around in circles for a short time and then bumped back on to the roadway.

John had exited his patrol car in order to get a better view of what was happening out in the field. When the truck bumped back on to the road, it headed directly toward John and his patrol car. John jumped on to the hood of his car to avoid being struck. When the truck passed by, he re-entered his car and marked back in pursuit.

A short distance away was the driveway to the plantation, and that is where the pickup truck headed. John announced the same on the police radio, and several police officers started in that direction. Mine was the third car to arrive at the residence, with two more to follow. John had stopped his car approximately two thirds of the way down the driveway. The two occupants of the truck had bailed out of the truck and fled into the residence.

The curtilage surrounding the house itself really was quite threatening, with so many places for someone to hide. Sturm was known to have big aggressive dogs at the rear of the residence. Ordinarily, I would have set up a perimeter of officers around the house, preventing escape from the rear. It just didn't seem like a good thing to do on that particular summer evening. Sturm and his buddy could be hiding anywhere on that property, waiting for an opportunity to attack. He had a bad reputation to begin with, and had just tried to run down a police officer and then fled.

As we crouched behind our police cars and close by oak trees, I instructed police communications to call the residence on the telephone, to establish contact. Shortly, the dispatcher radioed that the residential phone had been disconnected by the phone company for non-payment of bills.

I instructed one of the officers to get on his public address speaker, mounted on the roof of the police car, and call to the inside of the house for the residents to come out. After we called several times, the front door opened and Sturm's live-in girlfriend, Libby, stepped out onto the front porch with a small child beside her.

With numerous curse words interlaced in her speech, Libby asked why we, the police, were in her front yard. The immediate previous events were explained to her and we instructed Libby to approach our location with the child. Libby stepped down off of the front porch and started toward the police cars. Spotlights were trained on her and as she continued, she lifted her blouse, exposing her bare breasts and said, "See, I don't have a f------ weapon." Class act indeed.

Libby was taken into protective custody for the time being. The small child belonged to a neighbor, and Libby was babysitting the child. Wow!

Suddenly, the loud crack of a rifle shot rang out close by! Off to our collective left side a rifle had just been fired and someone was yelling, "I got one of the bastards, honey, I got one."

We had all hit the dirt hard when the blast happened. While Libby had provided a diversion on the front porch and yard, Sturm had sneaked out of the back of the house and low crawled into the front side field, directly adjacent to our location. Two officers testified later in court that they had heard the bullet of the 30.06 rifle whiz directly over their heads.

Immediately after the shot, I jumped up from the ground and got behind a mature oak tree (thank you plantation owner from the 1800s). The adrenaline was pumping so hard that my left foot was hopping up and down and would not hold still. I thought, 'Stop it!' and somehow got some control of the motor skills of my foot. I already had my shotgun in one hand because I didn't like the entire situation. Sturm was now 10 to 15 yards away from me, and I was the closest officer to him. He was jumping around and yelling about getting one of them. He was holding his rifle at his waist in a "ready gun" position, with the barrel pointing to his left, but, the gun was waving in an animated way in his hands and would turn slightly toward my location.

I had my shotgun pointed at his chest with slight pressure on the trigger. I was also holding a three-cell flashlight and the shotgun barrel grip in my left hand. But the three-cell light barely illuminated Sturm. Days before, I had read about a police "technical" flashlight with a halogen bulb, new technology at the time. I swore right then that I would make the $100+ purchase the very next day, and I did.

As Sturm was animatedly rotating that rifle barrel back and forth, I made up my mind to shoot him if the barrel jerked toward me. I yelled to Sturm to put his rifle down and he replied, "No, you put your rifle down!" I yelled back, "I can't, I am the police. You put yours down."

There is no accounting for what works and doesn't, but I guess the logic of what I had just said sunk in and Sturm squatted down and placed his rifle on the ground. As he stood up, I heard a high-pitched squeal and out of the corner of my eye saw John Atkisson launch himself and make a mid-body, open-field tackle of which any college or pro football player would be proud, and take Sturm to the ground.

Sturm was immediately swarmed by the other officers and was searched, hand-cuffed, and placed in a police car.

Knowing that there were two male occupants in the truck and that we had already been shot at once, I decided to search the house for safety purposes. Officer Kenny James and I entered the residence and searched room to room. While we were being as quiet as possible, we had to be making some amount of noise. As we entered the residence, we immediately turned to our right to search the front left room. Kenny had his police service revolver and flashlight in hand, and I had my shotgun and flashlight.

I opened the door, and Kenny entered to the left and I entered to the right. No one home. That was good. The adrenaline was still pumping, and we both were on high alert. We continued our search from room to room in that manner. The back right room had a curtain for a door, and we heard a TV playing from inside the room.

We jerked back the curtain and entered guns first. The second occupant of the errant truck was lying on the couch watching TV. He nearly jumped out of his skin as we made our dynamic entry. With all that had been going on outside, rifle shot included, I thought, how could he possibly be lying on the couch watching TV? I guess that drugs and alcohol can mask anything.

With the high amount of adrenaline that laced through my veins that night, it was a very long drive back to police headquarters. Everything was still in slowed motion. Everyone involved in that encounter that night was lucky, to include Jim Sturm. My police officers behaved bravely and with restraint. There were two rookie officers on the scene and one rookie sergeant – me. I thanked God for the help.

CHAPTER 16
LEARNING THE ROPES OF SUPERVISION
AND OF SAILING

WHILE WORKING THE PERMANENT EVENING SHIFT, my experience as a first-line street supervisor grew quickly, much more so than if I had been assigned to the midnight shift or even the day shift.

Evening shift roll call began sharply at 3 PM, 1500. Roll call required much preparation on supervision's part. A shift assignment schedule was made up five days in advance, subject to change at any time, to include the last minute. Responsibilities rotated within supervision from month to month, and one sergeant would be responsible for roll call preparation and presentation to the officers. Another supervisor would have to read and evaluate all reports generated by the shift at the end of the tour of duty. A third sergeant had to be on the street immediately after roll call, no matter what. Each sergeant had eight to twelve officers that he or she evaluated, but also was responsible for supervision of all officers working that evening. Sergeants were required to go to as many emergency calls and "hot" calls as possible during the shift. The sergeant was the scene supervisor unless relieved by a higher authority. That included all crimes, no matter how serious, and a young sergeant might well be supervising a detective or detectives on a robbery or homicide until a detective supervisor arrived.

New supervisors find out quickly that threats to their well-being come from within the organization as well as from without. Seemingly, every decision is evaluated or worse, "Monday morning quarterbacked." Too many inappropriate decisions would end a supervisor's career as a supervisor. The sergeants' standing mantra was "You are only as good as your last decision." The point of this is that while being a first-line street supervisor is exciting and rewarding, it is very stressful, particularly so if one is aspiring to rise higher in the organization.

I found a great stress reliever to be the sport and lifestyle of sailing. Teri and I were greatly excited about sailing our new-to-us, ten-year-old 1982 S-2 center cockpit sailboat, *Razzle Dazzle*.

Several years prior, Teri had taken a "learn to cruise" bare-boat sailing course and had earned a certificate allowing her to charter a bareboat. Thus, the first time that we took the boat out of the slip, Teri was at the helm. We had a glorious sail and we both knew that we had made the right decision in buying the boat. Upon returning to the slip, Teri took the helm again and proceeded to back the boat into the slip. The only problem was that she got a little too close to the boat in the next slip and slightly bumped the anchor that was mounted on the bow rail. The anchor, of course, swung back and forth a couple of times before it dropped from its mount and splashed into the creek. Cat calls and whistles came from across the marina and, needless to say, Teri was mortified.

After that incident, Teri refused to take the helm for several trips. For me, backing the boat into the slip was a mystery. I didn't understand that boats "walk" in one direction or the other. The boat had to approach the slip at a right angle as there was not enough room to back straight in. My attempts were grim.

Teri finally decided to take another try at it, and on her first attempt the boat entered the slip flawlessly, touching nothing. This happened every time thereafter. This became so funny because after several months of Teri entering the slip perfectly each time, longtime slip holders were asking her how to back in. Teri was a natural sailor. I closely mimicked her maneuvers and eventually I too could dock the boat without event.

CHAPTER 17
EXPENSIVE LESSON

IN AUGUST of that first sailing season I invited my wind-surfing buddy and close friend, Dave Enochs, to go sailing with me for a few days. Dave drove up from the Outer Banks of North Carolina, about a three and a half hour trip. We provisioned the boat and were ready for the adventure. The wind was blowing like stink, probably 20 to 25 knots, and it was hot, really hot, literally one hundred degrees mid-day.

I was still very new to sailing a monohull, but I was ready for our first great sailing adventure. We pulled out of the slip and motored down Broad Creek and out into the mighty Rappahannock River, where the wind was really howling. As soon as we got in clean air, it was more than evident that we needed to reef the mainsail and partially furl the jib. Had I known anything at all, I would have reefed the mainsail before leaving the dock, but I had never, ever reefed the boat at any time. When sailing the Hobie cat, we never reefed, we just sailed faster. When windsurfing, we didn't reef, we changed to a smaller sail for stronger wind.

At that time in my sailing career, I did not know enough to furl away the jib before trying to reef the main; thus, when we headed up into the wind to reef the main, the 140 percent Genoa protested mightily.

Dave and I began to claw down the mainsail to the first reefing point. Of course while in this maneuver, the main was flogging itself to death and we were struggling to hang on to the sail and keep the boat pointed into the wind.

At that exact moment, a batten shot out of the back of the mainsail and flew across the water, never to be seen again. I then noticed a tear in the batten pocket. I exclaimed, "Oh no, Teri is going to kick my butt!" This was the first time that I had taken the boat out without her and I had damaged the sail and lost a batten.

The plan was to sail up the Rappahannock to the Corrotoman River, where there were several nice anchorages for spending the night. The wind was blowing straight down the Rappahannock and, naturally, to get there we needed to go up the Rappahannock.

We did manage to reef the main after some trial and error, but we left the genoa fully deployed. On each tack of the boat, Dave complained that he was having great difficulty in sheeting in the genoa.

"What's the problem, are you a wimp or what," I thought. Finally, I had Dave take the helm, and when he tacked the boat I found out just what the problem was. Way too much sail to sheet in against the pressure of 20 to 25 knot wind.

I had been fast tacking the boat, flipping her around, and poor Dave had no chance to get any of the sheet in before the genoa filled with all of that wind pressure.

At about that time, Dave turned a really funny shade of green and allowed as how he didn't feel too well. The pure physical exertion, heat, and waves had gotten to Dave. He weakly said, "We can go home any time you like."

I knew that if I took Dave back to shore then, he would never set foot on that boat again. I had to somehow make this fun. We reduced sail, took longer tacks, and I slowly tacked the boat around, giving Dave time to sheet the sail before it filled.

As we slid under the Rappahannock River Bridge, the wind dropped out dramatically. The bridge does shadow the wind, but there was a wind shift and the wind lightened. Now we were able to sail on one tack and Dave, reclining on the leeward side, got in a good snooze. "Hey, when is it my turn?" I thought.

The day was wearing on and we had been drinking Gatorade regularly, but we never urinated, as we sweated out the liquid as fast as we took it in.

The entrance to the Corrotoman takes one to river left, or the west side of the river. From the Rappahannock, the entrance aids to navigation are pretty far away and difficult to see. My Dad had helped me install a Micrologic Loran receiver, and I used it and my Chesapeake Bay chartbook to find the marks. Every five minutes I transcribed the latitude and longitude (actually Loran time differentials) onto the chart in order to find my exact location. I didn't want to run aground, no matter what.

Finally as evening was drawing near, we closed in on our destination. I was ready to relax and enjoy the evening, even though the temperature was still in the upper nineties.

As we made our turn toward the destination, the river began to close down, and I felt a need to get the sails down immediately. When I pulled on the genoa furling line and Dave eased the working sheet, nothing happened. The sail did not begin to furl on to the extrusion. Clear water was diminishing. "I have to get this sail in," I thought.

I knew better than to do this, but I did it anyway: I placed the furling line onto a winch and began cranking with the winch handle. At first, it was very tight, hard to crank, then, BANG!, at the top of the mast.

"What was that?" Dave asked.

"I don't know, but, it can't be good," I replied.

It was now easy to furl in the genoa, and furl it I did. The main came down with no issue.

After setting the anchor for the night, I got out the binoculars and looked at the masthead. I could see something sticking straight out, something that shouldn't be there. The genoa halyard had broken at the top of the mast when I applied the winch to the furling line. As I said, I knew better, but I was desperate to get the sail furled.

I reluctantly called Yankee Point Marina on the marine VHF radio and explained my plight. They kindly replied that they would take a look at the damage the next morning, adding that, "Yes, the genoa would probably fall down if I chose to unfurl it."

"Now Teri is really going to kick my butt," I thought. It was still really hot and I wanted to jump into that Corrotoman River to cool down. One problem – there were so many jellyfish that we could have walked across them to shore. I asked Dave if he thought there was any way to get in the water without getting stung many times over. He looked at me as though I were from the moon. We got the bucket out and tied a line to it and lowered it overboard. Believe me when I say that we examined the contents very closely before pouring the water over our heads.

Budweiser and steaks were on the menu that evening, and I don't know when an ice-cold Budweiser ever tasted that good. When I crawled into the aft cabin that night, it was still ninety-seven degrees and the sweat was dripping off of me. "How will I possibly be able to sleep?" I thought. The next thing I knew, it was morning.

Yankee Point Marina repaired the halyard in short order and said that the halyard had wrapped itself around a kink in the forestay at the very top of the mast and that the forestay needed to be replaced. The kink had been identified in the pre-purchase survey, but it had been said that it could wait until the end of the season to be repaired. Indeed.

Dave and I had a fun and uneventful sail back down the Rappahannock to Deltaville and our home slip in Sting Ray Harbor Marina.

After discussing the issues with Teri, who did not kick my butt and was very understanding, we decided to take the boat back to Yankee Point Marina to have the forestay replaced to include a new furling system. We wanted to reward Yankee Point with our business for being so kind as to deal with my situation at a moment's notice. That trip turned out to be an adventure as well, but Yankee Point Marina did a fine job of the installation, which served the boat until she was sold in 1998.

CHAPTER 18
SAILING

FROM MARCH 1992 until May 2003, my various crew and I plied the waters of wonderful Chesapeake Bay on board a succession of sailboats – first, *Razzle Dazzle*, then *Summer Heat*, and, finally, *Southern Heat*.

Many weekend trips and at least one week-long trip annually were enjoyed on the bay. Our sailing skills grew quickly through reading and practical application. I never intentionally went out in bad or stormy weather but sometimes got caught out and was forced to deal with the situation at hand, thus gaining even more experience. We explored many wonderful destinations over the years, some only a couple of hours away and others several days distant.

We naturally started close to home port and anchored out for the first time in Indian Creek off of Fleets Bay, just north of the Rappahannock River. Teri had read about Indian Creek and Pittman's Cove and suggested that we give it a try.

It was quite exciting and challenging (at that time in my sailing experience) to sail out around Windmill Point and head into Fleets Bay. The aids to navigation seemed to be far apart and difficult, if not impossible, to see with the natural summer haze hanging in the air. I probably plotted the coordinates a hundred times on the chartbook, referring every 5 minutes or so to the Loran for information. The entrance to Indian Creek was really very straight forward with no navigational issues.

Pittman's Cove was, perhaps, one nautical mile up the creek on the left. The cove was smallish with protection from all sides. At the time, there were only several houses and many oak trees on shore. Pittman's Cove, to this day, remains my default place to anchor if I am in the area.

Another really exciting trip was to sail across the bay for the first time and spend the night, to return home the following day. Again, I relied on my Loran and chartbook to escort me to the far side of the bay, twenty nautical miles away and out of sight of land for quite a while. We "followed" another sailboat from our marina, and I learned that on the open water, boats lose visible contact with one another pretty quickly. But it was reassuring to know that the other boat was up there ahead of us somewhere.

As I learned, the Chesapeake has many faces, and she can change those faces quickly. We had a fantastic sail across the bay to the town of Onancock on the Eastern Shore of Virginia. We experienced blue sky, two foot waves, and 10 to 15 knots on the beam – perfect.

The following morning we awoke to 15 to 20 knots out of the northeast, which produced a nasty following sea for the thirty-foot sloop and relatively inexperienced crew at the time.

One crew member had celebrated the crossing a little too much the previous night and felt pretty awful for the return wallowing trip. That crew member volunteered to ride the bus home from the Eastern Shore. I don't know if a bus even ran from Onancock or not, but I said "No way, you have to help me sail this boat back." There was a great deal of motion with the following sea pushing the boat around, but the trip was uneventful. One more notch in the sailing experience.

We routinely sailed to Indian Creek, the Corrotoman River, Urbana, Virginia (sixteen nautical miles up the Rappahannock), the Great Wicomico and the Piankatank. Within a couple of years we expanded greatly: the Potomac River, Colonial Beach, Tangier Sound and Tangier Island, Crisfield, MD., the Patuxent River and Solomon's Island, the middle bay and Annapolis, Baltimore, St. Michaels, and Oxford, Maryland.

CHAPTER 19
DEADLY EXPLOSION

I HAVE CHOSEN to tell sailing stories with a twist of some sort, generally some mishap or uncomfortable situation that lends itself to interesting reading. But the vast majority of my sailing trips have been just plain fun, stress-relieving good times. Some sparkled with fantastic days of sailing, but uneventful in any negative sort of way. The law enforcement stories are generally ones of dangerous encounters, which have led to even a stronger desire to get out on the water to get away. They also helped prepare me for emergencies on the water, as did the many things that I learned in the Boy Scouts and four years in the U.S. Army.

One such case happened early in my law-enforcement career. As Sergeant Joe Friday of the TV show "Dragnet" would say, "I was working the evening shift" on Jefferson Davis Highway (U.S. Route I and 301) in the southern part of Chesterfield County.

It was possible to go home for a quick bite to eat, if one lived close by, and that is what I had done. This was very infrequent for me as it was always stressful for my wife to try to guess when I might actually get there and equally stressful for me to try to honor that commitment. I could be pulling into the driveway and get another call for service.

I had just finished eating and heard an emergency call on my hand-held police-frequency scanner that my mother had bought for me. This was before the days of each officer having his/her own hand-held radio.

"BEEEEP" the emergency tones were emitted. "Chesterfield to all units, an explosion has occurred at the Dutch Gap VEPCO (Virginia Power) station. Units to respond?"

I said, "Bye, gotta go," to Teri and ran out of the door to my police car. The power station was about one mile from my home and I would be the closest officer to the scene. I activated my red lights (at that time; now they're blue) and siren and marked "in route" on the radio.

Information coming in from the police radio dispatcher was spotty, but I received the following, "Unit 111, (my unit number at the time), respond to the main VEPCO gate and someone will be there to escort you to the actual scene." I responded, "Unit 111, 10-4."

The route to the power plant had several twists and turns and a railroad crossing to negotiate. I made the best time that I could and arrived at the front gate within minutes. The VEPCO employee was waiting for me and led me around to the far side of the plant. He looked as though he was shell shocked and said that there had been an explosion of a large circuit breaker and that one man was dead and others were hurt. I quickly radioed in that one victim was possibly deceased and there were injuries to others. I was still a new officer and in my haste and excitement I used the ten code for suicide rather than deceased subject. The police dispatcher figured out what I really meant.

The escort led me into the plant, which was darkened, smoke-filled, and loud. As we moved along, I looked down to see my footing and could see lights one or two levels below me, through the grating that served as the floor. Unnerving. When we approached the explosion area, it looked as though we were entering Dante's Hell. No kidding. What I have already described was bad enough, but then I saw fire and a red-orange glow billowing out of what was left of a huge, story-high circuit breaker. The deceased victim was about ten feet away, face down, with his arms folded under his chest, supporting his torso. His entire body was charred black and blood was slowly dripping from his nose.

We moved on to the control room and I found the shift supervisor, who was peppered with shrapnel from the explosion and somewhat disoriented but basically coherent. He told me that the deceased employee had been working on the circuit breaker when it exploded. The explosion literally threw him through the air. The supervisor had been standing nearby. According to the supervisor, all other employees were now outside the building, and we both felt a strong urge to get out of there, too. As I walked back past the dead body, Officer Mike Marion was administering CPR to him. This was a very futile effort, but Mike had to try.

As we all exited the plant, Detective Duncan Beasley was just arriving. One of his specialties was arson, not that this was arson, but Duncan knew his way around fire scenes and explosions. He asked if all employees were accounted for and I told him what the shift supervisor had told me.

"We need to verify that everyone is accounted for!" he said.

A duty roster was housed inside the control room, so in we went for the second time. I really did not want to go back into "hell," but I went with him. The shift supervisor located the duty roster and verified the location of everyone. I was very glad to get back out side again.

One of the injured employees turned out to be a neighbor who lived down the street from me and he received severe hand injuries. I sometimes thought of the dead body with the blood dripping from the nose, but I did not let it haunt me.

CHAPTER 20
WEAR THE HAT

I LEARNED A GREAT DEAL in the first couple of years as a patrol officer, and one of the main things was to follow the rules and that the rules are there for a reason. The same holds true for sailing. Following the rules of sailing has served me well over the years.

As a young police officer, I only wore my police hat when it was not inconvenient. If I pulled into a convenience store parking lot to run inside for a soft drink, I might not bother with the hat. I usually wore it when I thought I was on official business. My sergeant found me twice without my hat and admonished me to always have that thing on my head except when driving the car.

After the second incident, I began wearing the hat any time that I exited the car, but the infractions showed up on my annual evaluation. I was upset, but the sergeant was right – it took two warnings to get my attention.

There are many reasons for wearing the hat: It is part of the uniform; it requires compliance of each officer; it gives the officer more of an official look; it makes the officer look bigger; and it helps other officers identify each other as being police officers and not a possible assailant coming around the corner.

Early in my career, one night on the midnight shift, I had effected a traffic stop for a possible DUI (driving under the influence).

Generally, officers back one another on DUI traffic stops, but no one showed up that night. The suspect vehicle had been weaving on the highway and his speed was erratic, speeding up and slowing down. This occurred on a two-lane highway with no traffic at around 2 a.m.

I activated my red lights and marked on the radio that I was effecting a traffic stop for possible DUI and gave the location. The vehicle pulled over to the road side and I exited my vehicle, remembering to don my hat, place my twenty-four-inch baton in its belt holder, and bring my flashlight.

I approached the vehicle on foot, and the suspect exited the driver's side door. He had an odor of alcoholic beverage on his breath, his speech was slightly slurred, and he had a bit of swaying to his motion. As I conducted my investigation of his condition, the driver vacillated between being jovial to angry, back and forth. That is typical of someone who has had too much to drink.

I administered several coordination tests, finger to nose, stand on one foot and hold one's balance, walk a straight line for a certain number of steps and turn around and walk back a certain number of steps, count from ten to one, and "say your ABCs."

He performed poorly on all tests, missing his nose with his finger, swaying when walking in a non-straight line, unsteady on one foot, counting backward slowly, but, accurately, and stumbling through his ABCs. During the tests, his mood became increasingly less friendly with a touch of surliness thrown in.

I placed the suspect under arrest, handcuffed his hands behind his back, placed him in the police car and transported him to police headquarters for a breathalyzer test. Ultimately, he blew above the legal limit on the breathalyzer and I took him before a magistrate to state my probable cause for the arrest, obtain the arrest warrant and incarcerate him for the night.

The magistrate always asked the suspect for a statement, or his version of the incident. The suspect said that my assessment of the night was about right, but that "if the officer had not been so big, I would have kicked his ass."

At the time, I stood six feet tall and weighed all of 155 pounds. The suspect was taller and weighed substantially more than did I. I am convinced that wearing the police hat that night saved me from rolling around in the ditch with the suspect. Without a doubt, the hat made me look taller, more official, unapproachable, and somewhat threatening. Thank you, Sergeant Terrell, for teaching me to follow the rules. I was pretty rule-oriented anyway, but he firmed up the soft spot.

In my own supervisory and management years, I always encouraged officers to wear the hat and enforced the rule for noncompliance. Some officers did not like to wear their hats to domestic situations, but that is the precise situation in which the hat serves the officer very well. Once control of the situation has been gained, it might be appropriate to remove the hat and sit down at the kitchen table with the distraught couple to sort things out, but not until things are really under control.

As a supervisor, I have walked into the front yard of a family in domestic crisis more than once and found the responding officer(s) to be hatless and hear the male resident respond to the officer as "hey buddy" or words to that effect. When I approached with the head gear in place, the same male resident would refer to me as officer or sir. I guess the rules really are there for a reason.

What we do not know is how many times over the years that the uniformed person has served to establish control or maintain control in any given situation, where a potential assailant has sized up the officer, recognizing that he or she is squared away, maintaining self-discipline and probably not someone to challenge. We do know of specific times that the demeanor, presence, and appearance all come in to play to maintain order. I have just illustrated two examples. A third comes to mind.

Again, late in the evening, I had executed a traffic stop for suspected DUI and placed the driver under arrest for the same. Ironically, when I activated the emergency lights, the driver had pulled into the parking lot of one of the roughest drinking establishments on Jefferson Davis Highway, the Raven Inn, a renowned biker bar.

Normally, when a DUI arrest is effected, the motorist's vehicle will be towed away for safe keeping until the owner sobers up and is released from jail. On this particular occasion, the driver had pulled onto private property and not the road side. He was cooperative and I wanted to save him a tow bill if I could. I asked him if he wanted his car towed for safe keeping or if he would like to leave it in the parking lot at the Raven Inn. He requested to leave his car in the lot. I had a volunteer police officer riding with me that night so I left the special officer with the arrestee and I entered the Raven to talk with the owner/operator of the bar about the possibility of leaving the car there for the night.

When I entered the Raven I saw two or three patrons, one at the bar and one or two sitting at tables in the lowly lit room. The owner was off to the left side of the bar, some distance from the patron. I explained the situation to the owner and he said that it would be alright to leave the vehicle in his parking lot overnight. I thanked him and turned to walk out of the front door. After taking several steps I heard "Fu----- pig!"

I had a choice: I could ignore the comment and walk out the door, or I could confront the patron at the bar who had made the utterance. He had broken no law, but he had crossed the line and laid down a challenge in his comfort zone, in front of a couple of his peers. If I walk out, nothing bad happens – except that the Chesterfield police have now implicitly backed down from a Raven Inn patron. That can't happen.

I made sure that my good old police hat was about one inch off of my nose and I turned around and with deliberate steps, walked up to the drunk at the bar. I had my hat brim about six inches from his forehead and asked in a low voice "What did you say?"

"I didn't say nothing."

"That's what I thought," I said and turned around and walked out.

CHAPTER 21
STURM FOR THE LAST TIME

MY LAST ENCOUNTER with the infamous Jim Sturm occurred shortly after Jim Bourque was promoted to lieutenant and transferred to the evening shift as the new shift lieutenant.

Sturm called the emergency services communications center and said that he was despondent and had been drinking and ingested a number of meds. The call was transferred to the sergeants' office and Sgt. Jim Stanley took the call.

After talking with Sturm for a while, Sgt. Stanley believed that Sturm probably had taken enough drugs and alcohol to put his life in danger. Doing the right thing, Sgt. Stanley appeared before a magistrate and stated his probable cause to obtain a mental deficiency warrant for Sturm.

Sgt. Stanley was going off duty early that evening, and the task of supervising the serving of the warrant fell on my shoulders. I brought the new lieutenant up to speed on the department's previous dealings with Sturm. I, personally, had come within seconds, twice, of shooting the man.

"Let me think about it for a minute," Lt. Bourque said.

Shortly after, he called me back in to his office and proposed a plan of action that I thought was great. It went like this.

First, I contacted the volunteer rescue squad that worked Sturm's area of the county and explained what we had. They agreed to stand by at the far end of Sturm's driveway and wait for me to call them in for an approach to the residence.

Several officers and I responded to the residence with warrant in hand. I sent Officer Lorie Smith to the rear of the residence, and two big officers and I positioned ourselves on the front porch, walking very quietly so as not to alert Sturm. We listened for any sound coming from within the residence, but all was quiet.

I contacted the rescue squad via radio and had them drive down the driveway to the front of the residence, quietly and without lights of any kind. I then had police communications call the residence on the phone. Sturm had obviously had his phone service re-activated since the last incident. We could hear the phone ringing inside the residence, in the right front bedroom. We heard Sturm answer the phone and speak to the police dispatcher, who told Sturm that the rescue squad was in front of his residence to offer any needed help. At that point I had the rescue squad activate their red emergency lights. Sturm would see the red flashing lights of the rescue vehicle, not the blue lights of a police car.

We stood away from the windows and saw Sturm peek out from the window shade to see who or what was really out there. Our plan was to grab Sturm as soon as he opened the door and stepped on to the porch. Sturm came to the door and began unlocking numerous locks. I whispered "Get ready," and my two large officers were prepared for the physical confrontation.

Sturm opened the door, but only partially, and the first officer quickly slammed his body against the door and the other officer hit it a half-second later, forcing the door to open and Sturm to stumble backward.

Sturm yelled, "What thu, what thu, what are you people doing here?"

All three of us were grabbing for Sturm's arms and torso to get him restrained as quickly as possible. Sturm was stumbling backwards and to his left in an effort to retreat. The mass of collective bodies entered the left front room together with Sturm starting to fall backward into the center of the room. We crashed into a free-standing wood stove, which, fortunately, was not in use. The stove collapsed and the group fell to the floor in the darkened room with the struggle continuing. I had one arm and was trying to force it to the center of

Sturm's body. One my fellow officers yelled, "He's got a knife and he is cutting me!" "Damn!" I thought. "Got to get this stopped!"

I yelled for Lorie Smith to come in and help. She must have already been moving toward us from the rear of the house because she appeared quickly. Sturm was on his back and the three of us were all around him, struggling to gain control. Officer Smith ran into the room and with one well-placed kick, took the fire right out of Jim Sturm. I am just glad that her kick was accurate as we were all vulnerable to an errant foot. The knife turned out to be Sturm's long finger nails, which he was using as weapons against my police officer.

Jim Sturm never called the Chesterfield County Police again. Several months later, he did call the Virginia State Police, and when the troopers arrived Sturm said that the last time he called the Chesterfield police, "They came out here and kicked my ass!" Shortly after that, Sturm moved out of the county.

CHAPTER 22
POSITIVE CONTACTS

NOT ALL CONTACTS with the public were negative, particularly after getting into supervision and management. As I said earlier, shortly after being promoted to the rank of sergeant, I was transferred to the Safety and Community Support Unit. I began seeing the good side of our citizens and heard their concerns about their own safety. It was rewarding to make crime prevention/public safety presentations to neighborhood groups and community organizations as well as to children of all ages.

Upon completion of that tour of duty, I returned to uniformed operations and worked the evening shift as a shift sergeant. One evening, I had just finished my evening meal and was walking toward my patrol car from the restaurant when I heard from behind me, "Look Jimmy, there is a police officer!"

I turned around and saw a young mother and father with their little boy of about five years of age. As I walked toward them, the young mother said, "My son just loves police officers." I squatted down to little Jimmy's level and said, "Hi, my name is Sergeant Hope, what is yours?"

I extended my hand, and he shyly shook it. I asked him if he would like to see my police car and looked up at his mother to see if that would be ok. Jimmy beamed with a great big grin and shook his head up and down in the affirmative. We walked over to the unmarked car and I opened the door and had him sit in the passenger seat. I showed him all of the gadgets inside the car, and then had him exit the vehicle. I told Jimmy to cover his ears and that I would activate the siren for him and turn on the blue lights. After we talked for a few minutes, it was time for Jimmy and his parents to leave, as they were en route home to one of the far northern states.

This was a very easy gesture on my part, as I had performed numerous "Officer Friendly" programs in my previous .assignment. I was not in a hurry to go anywhere and it cost nothing to be nice to that little boy and his parents. At the time, I did not know that they were not Chesterfield County residents, but it would not have mattered anyway. I went on about my shift and thought no more about the encounter. A month or two later, I received a copy of a letter that had been written to Chief Pittman. It was from Jimmy's mother who said what a positive experience it had been to have Sgt. Hope take time out of his busy night to talk with her little boy. It was the nicest letter, which she certainly did not have to write. My small act meant so much to her, the letter brought tears to my eyes and still does today.

Time moved on, and sailing and windsurfing had taken first and second place in my leisure-time pursuits. My time was divided between driving to the Outer Banks of North Carolina to windsurf, a three-and-a-half-hour trip, and driving one and three quarter hours to Deltaville to sail on our sailboat. Windsurfing was my first choice, but the boat often won out due to the shorter trip.

At some point, it didn't matter to me as long as I was on the water. Teri and I learned to sail in stronger winds and we often went out when many others elected to stay in port. Experience was mounting up. Teri and I would take a week's vacation on the boat and another week at the beach. The third week was split into a day here and there, usually at the boat for a long weekend.

Dave Enochs sailed with me for a week at a time for a number of years during the mid to late 1990s. One particular year, on three separate occasions, when I was actually on the water, there were drownings within ten to fifteen miles of my location. All three times involved overloaded 17-foot open bow fishing boats that were out in windy conditions. On numerous occasions, I saw small boats in three- to four-foot chop, a very unnecessary risk.

CHAPTER 23
POLICE LIEUTENANT

PROFESSIONALLY, things were looking up. I suffered through another promotional process and on November 1, 1989, I was promoted to the rank of lieutenant and I knew that I was on my way! I was assigned to Uniformed Operations Bureau, north district, evening shift. The transition was less difficult than it could have been as I had been assigned to the same shift as a street sergeant for the past four years. Chesterfield police officers wear forest green uniforms, but at the time lieutenants and above wore white shirts. I had become one of the "white shirts," also known as "one of them," and no longer "one of us."

The transition was shockingly immediate. The evening shift, north district was now mine, not someone else's. The ultimate decision making and responsibility fell squarely on my shoulders.

"Be careful for what you ask, you might get it," were never truer words. When I put on my white uniform shirt for the first time I was stunned at how bright it was. The darn thing glowed it was so bright. That afternoon at 1500, I walked from the rear of the roll call room to the front to speak for the first time to my shift as their shift commander. As I moved forward, the evening shift officers broke out into hearty applause, not just polite clapping. I was honored and humbled. Now I had to live up to their expectations and that of upper management, as well and the citizens of Chesterfield County.

It is funny how things change so quickly. That first evening, I went on a felony warrant service call with several of my officers. Keep in mind that I had been one of their immediate supervisors for the last four years. Prior to walking up to the residence, we had met in a field close by. It was dusk and getting darker. After making an action plan, it was time to make our approach on foot. Seasoned officers who went with me anywhere the night before, walked away from me as quickly as they could to avoid being near that glowing white shirt. What a target! It was a symbolic target too. Citizens knew the difference between regular patrol officers and those wearing white shirts and gravitated to the white shirt, especially if they did not like what the patrol officer had to say.

A great deal of pressure came with the unit commander or shift commander position. The "Monday morning quarter-backing" grew exponentially from that of being a sergeant. As a shift lieutenant, I supervised five sergeants and thirty-some patrol officers. Anything that any one of them did, good or not so good, landed at my feet. Of course my own decisions were evaluated daily. To add to the stress, my captain was promoted at the same time as I was and transferred to the Uniform Operations Bureau after his many years in covert operations. He was on a steep learning curve and was a man who wanted to do the very best that he could. He managed all three of the north district shifts, the marine patrol, the K-9 squad and the crash team.

Every weekday immediately after roll call, I had the pleasure of meeting with my captain, who often had recently gotten off of the phone with some irate citizen. I received the brunt of his frustration from listening to the citizen's rant. After a number of these unpleasant meetings, I reminded the captain that there are always two sides of a story and asked him to please let me get some answers before assuming that the first side that he heard was the correct one. To his credit, he agreed, and the meetings became less confrontational. Again, to his credit, he held my toes to the fire, but went to bat for me when he thought I was right. He never offered me up as a sacrificial lamb. My leadership style was quite different from his and from his boss's. After a time, I learned to really trust the captain and the converse of that, he learned to trust me. We learned a lot together.

A great deal of paperwork was involved with the position of shift commander, but the lieutenant was still expected to spend as much time on the road as possible. Many various reports came across my desk or were generated at my desk. The ones that caused me the most concern were Office of Professional Standards investigations; in other words, internal affairs.

"Minor" complaints, those that would not cause lost pay, demotion, or termination of employment, were often assigned to and investigated at the shift level. A patrol officer's immediate supervisor, his sergeant, would conduct the investigation. The sergeant was responsible for making a recommendation of founded, not founded, or not sustained as well as a recommendation for corrective measures, if any. Once completed, the investigation would go to the shift commander for his/her review and then up the chain of command. These investigations were given the utmost attention and highest level of seriousness.

Serious decisions were made nightly, often between a sergeant and the lieutenant as to a course of action on a high-risk case. If the S.W.A.T. team needed to be called, a sergeant could take that responsibility but deferred to a lieutenant if one were working. The lieutenant would be involved in any high-risk warrant service that would happen on his shift, no matter who was serving it. As with the sergeants, the shift commander would respond to as many high-profile calls as possible.

All levels had the opportunity to serve on various committees, all of which met during regular 8 to 5 work hours. It did not matter to what shift one was assigned; you were expected to attend your committee meetings.

I served as a shift commander (lieutenant) for approximately four years. Many serious incidents happened both on and off the street while I served in that capacity. I dealt with cases such as S.W.A.T. call outs, vehicular pursuits, shootings, homicides, suicides, serious domestics, bank robberies, burglaries, home invasions, drug cases, lost children or elderly adults, traffic fatalities and/or serious injuries, police vehicle accidents, officer injuries, and police-involved shootings, to name the most common.

A common mistake is to think that a shift lieutenant never gets directly involved in street incidents. The thing is that the lieutenant should be responding to serious calls for service. He should let his officers work the case, but what if he gets there first or encounters someone leaving the scene?

I was involved directly in several vehicular pursuits as a shift commander since I was responding to the call for service and the event popped up right in front of me. One particular Sunday evening, I was having supper at a favorite Chinese restaurant with one of my sergeants, Sgt. Rick Reid. We had been monitoring a call for service for some time, involving a teenage driver who took his mother's car without permission. In essence, he had stolen the car. He had returned to his home and shoved his mother around, constituting an assault. Officers had been to the residence at least twice and were actively looking for the suspect and the vehicle.

As we were finishing our meal, an update came across the police hand-held radio that said that the suspect had obtained a shotgun and was responding to his home, his mother's home.

As we left the restaurant, I said to Rick, "It's about time for us to go find the bastard." Rick adamantly agreed. He jumped in his car and went in one direction and I went the other, both headed toward the complainant's residence.

As I drove down Robious Road I saw a car coming toward me that fit the description of the stolen car. Sure enough, as the car passed by my unmarked police car, I could see a young teenage white male behind the wheel. He had two passengers with him, one male and one female. I marked on the radio that I had the suspect vehicle in my sight and executed a road turn in order to follow him. As I was turning, he pulled into a 7-11 store and pulled up at the gas pump. I parked in a manner in which I hoped he would not see me and I hoped to apprehend the suspect as he returned to the vehicle from inside the store. Unfortunately, he saw me before I could get to him and he jumped into the car and sped off. I marked "in pursuit" on the radio and followed.

One-quarter mile away, the suspect turned into a mobile home trailer park. Fortunately, the park streets had numerous speed bumps and the suspect could not get his speed up. With blue lights, headlights flashers and siren going, I updated police communications of our rolling location. The suspect made a loop through the mobile home park and exited back onto Robious Road, west bound, toward his mother's home. By then Sgt. Reid and a female police officer were close by. I instructed them to establish a road block at the next intersection. They complied, but had to pull away as the suspect barreled toward the police cars, showing no sign of slowing or changing course. We were obligated to provide a "way out" for the vehicle that we were pursuing.

The patrol officer was able to immediately jump into the pursuit and took up first position behind the suspect, per policy; I was second, and Sgt. Reid was third in line. The suspect turned into a residential area and I felt the need to stop him immediately. I passed the patrol car and pulled alongside the suspect vehicle, and the teenage driver looked over at me, grinned and shot me the bird, his middle finger. This did nothing to help my attitude toward him.

He immediately swerved his vehicle toward my police car and I veered to the left to avoid contact. He moved back to the right and I moved to the right. He swerved at me again, and again I avoided collision. By then, Rick was directly behind me and the other patrol car was directly behind the suspect vehicle. Excellent; time for a rolling road block.

I accelerated rapidly and pulled in front of the suspect vehicle, and Sgt. Reid blocked him from the left. A high curb had him boxed in from the right. All three police cars began slowing, to make a controlled stop. The suspect swerved at Sgt. Reid's vehicle and made contact. The gloves were off. Rick turned into the suspect vehicle and we all came to a stop.

Knowing that there was supposed to be a shotgun in the vehicle, we should have executed a high-risk approach, but I knew that the driver could not get out of his side of the car as Rick's car was against his. I ran around the front of my car to the suspect's vehicle, where I pulled out the male and female passengers. What I really wanted was the driver; the adrenalin was really flowing through my veins. He had a death grip on the steering wheel and would not let go. It took about ten to fifteen seconds to make him let go, and we took him out of the vehicle and placed him on the ground, face down for control and to execute a search of his person.

I called the south district lieutenant to respond to the scene to investigate the damage to the police car and the suspect vehicle, since no supervisor at the scene could investigate it due to their own involvement. When Lt. Warner Williams arrived on the scene, he could see that Sgt. Reid was obviously nervous. Rick was worried about somehow getting into trouble for the damage to the cars. Warner, at first, thought we were hiding some fact from him, due to Rick's demeanor, but after explaining what happened several times,

Warner understood and Rick calmed down. The bottom line was that no one got hurt and we stopped further actions from the suspect. Ironically, the next day, Monday, the boy and his mother complained about the damage to mom's car.

CHAPTER 24
CLOSE ENCOUNTER

As TIME MOVED ON, spring, summer, and fall of each year became more and more sailboat oriented for Teri and me, with as much time as possible being spent on the Chesapeake Bay doing destination sailing. My days off from work rotated through the week, so when Teri and I did not have time off together I would head down to the Outer Banks for some fast windsurfing or to try to find someone to go with me on a sailing trip on the Chesapeake. The windsurfing and the sailing kept building my sailing experience.

By that time, I was an experienced police lieutenant who was looking toward a promotion to captain. I was commanding the evening shift, north district, and one particular evening I had left the office at 1900, or 7 PM, after finishing as much paperwork as I could stand.

Police headquarters was located in the south district but fairly centrally in the county. I was driving en route to the north district and thinking about finding somewhere to eat supper. Evening was approaching, but it was not dark yet. As I drove north on Chippenham Parkway, a four-lane, divided highway at the time, I was doing the speed limit, 55 mph, not in a hurry to get anywhere. Driving along, I was monitoring the traffic on the police radio, watching the vehicular traffic, and observing the overall setting in which I found myself. Traffic was light with a few vehicles in the south-bound lanes and only a Jeep Grand Wagoneer in the right-hand northbound lane a few car lengths in front of me.

Suddenly, without warning, there was a loud, violent explosion of impact directly in front of me. My mind struggled to interpret what was happening. A small "K-car" was literally flying toward me from the right-hand lane and crossed immediately in front of my car while airborne at a 45 degree attitude.

I saw the dark mass of the underside of the vehicle as it passed by my field of vision. The car was canted to its right but still right side up. As this imminent threat of death was approaching and passing by me, I jerked the steering wheel hard to the right and then back to the left, effectively dodging the car and it passed by at about 45 degrees apparent.

I was now in the right-hand lane with the Grand Wagoneer in front of me. "Whew, I made it!" I thought to myself. Then, "On no, the Wagoneer has lost speed and I am going to eat him up."

The Jeep had dramatically lost speed due to the head-on collision with the K-car. I was running out of room quickly. I jumped on the breaks and the ABS system did its job, preventing the car from skidding and I managed to keep it in a straight line. My police car came to an abrupt stop, inches from the rear bumper of the Jeep.

I quickly radioed in what had just happened and then ran back to the K-car, which had rolled to a stop 20 or so yards behind me. It was a crumpled mess. The driver, a young white female, had been crammed between the two front bucket-style seats and forced into the rear seat area of the vehicle. There was no more front seat area. The front end of the car now resided in what used to be the driver and front passenger area. The young woman was very obviously dead, with her body in a contorted position, her neck certainly broken.

Then, as I trotted forward to the Jeep to check on the people there, I radioed in that there was one fatality for sure. At the Jeep I found one middle-aged white woman to be the driver and no passengers. She was out of the vehicle and walking around. It was amazing, the K-car was totally destroyed and the Grand Wagoneer suffered a crumpled left front fender and some hood damage. The driver was shaken but did not display any physical injuries. Ironically, she had been en route to visit her husband in the hospital.

The immediate threat had happened in slow motion, but my mind was in warp speed. As I stood there with the driver of the Jeep, things began to slow down again. The adrenalin had been racing through my veins. I could hear the multiple sirens in the distance, a very welcome sound. While the struggle was over, it seemed like ages before help arrived.

Traffic fatalities are always significant events, and this time a police lieutenant was very nearly a part of it. Lots of help quickly arrived. Both northbound lanes had to be blocked, and traffic was diverted to one of the southbound lanes. That required a great deal of coordination. The crash team, of course, conducted the investigation. My boss's boss, Uniform Operations Bureau Commander Major Dennis McDonald arrived on the scene as he had just finished up an evening meeting. We had gone through the police academy together and were long-term friends, not that it matters in a professional encounter. Maj. McDonald stayed for a while, and right before he left, he told Sgt. Rick Reid to keep an eye on me for the rest of the shift. Dennis knew what I had just experienced and he wanted to make sure that I was OK mentally.

The Chesterfield Police Crash Team members take their job very seriously and are extremely thorough in their investigations of traffic accidents. This case was no exception. We knew at the scene that the K-car had proceeded the wrong way down the four-lane, divided highway with no headlights on. It was not dark, but dusky enough that the driver should have had her lights on. A witness who was good enough to return to the accident scene told the crash team investigators that he had been at the next crossover intersection and noticed the K-car because she had to make a difficult turn to accomplish it, enter the north-bound off ramp and head south in the north-bound, right hand lane. She accelerated rapidly and two or three cars veered out of her way.

Several days later it was learned that the young woman had been released from a mental-health facility just the weekend before the crash. Upon getting out, she told her private counselor that she just wanted to run head-long into a truck and end it all. She accomplished her wish. The woman in the Jeep should thank God that she was in such a durable vehicle. I know that if I had a teenager, the Grand Wagoneer would be the vehicle I would choose for my offspring. It's too bad that Jeep does not offer that vehicle any longer. I did thank God for sparing the other driver and me.

Maj. McDonald, later Deputy Chief McDonald, was correct to tell Sgt. Reid to keep an eye on me for the remainder of the shift. After leaving the accident scene, a call was dispatched that a woman was threatening suicide via handgun and that she had been drinking. I really did not need any more excitement for the night, but there it was.

Several officers responded to the residence, as did Sgt. Reid and I. We peeked through the curtains and saw the woman passed out on the couch, but we did not see the handgun. Was it under her, within an instant's touch? We did not know. How passed out was she? Was she in any risk of dying? If we forced the door open, would she wake up and pull out the gun? Rick and I discussed our options for a while before rushing into something that did not need to be rushed.

A sister had a key to the front door, and we had her respond to the scene with the key. The woman had never stirred. We decided to use the key to enter the residence and gain control of the woman. Still we wondered, would she wake up? As gently and quietly as possible, Rick slipped the key into the lock and turned it. He slowly and deliberately opened the door, and he and two officers entered. They gained control of the woman before she awoke. The handgun was under her body. God was with us again. That night it was another long drive back to the office, with the adrenalin winding down. I think I may have had a Jack Daniels or two when I got home that night. Usually, I went straight to bed, but not this time.

CHAPTER 25
THAT CHINESE RESTAURANT AGAIN

MANY EXCITING AND DANGEROUS INCIDENTS occurred during my eight years on the evening shift, both as a sergeant and as the shift lieutenant. The last story that I would like to relate follows.

Once again, I was having the evening meal at my favorite Chinese restaurant on Route 60. On this occasion, the south district shift commander, Lt. Warner Williams, had joined me. We worked, at the most, two common days together per week, he in the south and I in the north. We tried to meet for dinner to share notes on the events of the police department.

As we were leaving the restaurant, a call came across the radio stating that at an apartment complex just down the road a couple of miles, a suicidal subject was sitting on the hood of his vehicle with a gun in his mouth. This is the type of call to which a shift commander would respond.

I told Warner that I needed to head in that direction. He replied, "Dave, that's the kind of call that I will most likely be responding to anyway, so I may as well go along."

Warner was the S.W.A.T. commander at that time, and he was right. There was no reason for him to drive back to the south district, as he would probably be called right back up to the north district on the potential S.W.A.T. call out.

We found our way to the apartment complex and pulled into one end of the very large parking lot. One or two patrol officers were already present. As I visually scanned the parking lot I located the suspect, who was sitting on the hood of his car with a revolver in his hand. The lot was directly across from several apartment buildings, all of which faced the parking lot.

I exited my vehicle, and as I crouched down behind the driver's-side front wheel, the suspect put the barrel of the revolver into his mouth. I fully expected to see the back of his head explode within the next few seconds. Fortunately, he did not pull the trigger, but he kept that gun barrel in his mouth.

This was an untenable situation. The area was susceptible to pedestrian traffic from the apartments and the surrounding grounds as well as drive-up traffic coming into the complex. We had to contain the suspect and not let him go mobile, either on foot or in his vehicle. We also had to secure the area as best as we could. Should we try to evacuate the immediate apartments across from the suspect or have them secure themselves in the back rooms of their apartments? Establishing contact with the suspect was difficult too, as we did not want to get so close to him as to escalate the situation, but we needed to be close enough to "talk" with him and be able to respond toward him if necessary. As individual officers arrived on the scene, they were directed to establish a perimeter around the suspect. Some officers were deployed behind cars in the parking lot and some in the woods behind the lot. When the S.W.A.T. members began to arrive, they replaced the regular patrol officers on the perimeter and those officers established an outer perimeter. It is a particularly dangerous time in any situation that requires special teams, since everyone is vulnerable during this transition time.

With all of this to deal with, I was crouched behind my police car with the sweat, not perspiration, just plain old sweat, running down the inside of my protective vest and I thought, "Damn, it's hot." It was a summer night in central Virginia.

We did cautiously move a few families out of their apartments and warned the rest to take shelter in place in the rear rooms of their apartments. The officers who had to make those notifications and escort family members away were in harm's way, as they were totally exposed while involved in those tasks.

In the meantime, communications had been established with the suspect, who would take the gun from his mouth long enough to respond to the police negotiator and then place the barrel back in his mouth. After several hours of negotiations, the police negotiator convinced the suspect to relinquish his weapon and surrender to the team. I am sure that every officer on the scene that evening had to determinedly stay focused on the task at hand and not think about the oppressive heat.

CHAPTER 26
CHANGES

DURING THIS PERIOD, life was taking its toll and changes were beginning to happen all around me. Teri had finally gotten off of the midnight shift at Phillip Morris after twelve years and was assigned to the evening shift. We were, at last, on the same shift, although our days off hardly ever coincided. Even when we had days off together, Teri was often required to work compulsory overtime, thus eliminating the day off. For three years, the only time that we had off together was when we took vacation.

We had bought a travel trailer, which was located on a permanent site at the KOA campground in Rodanthe on the Outer Banks of North Carolina. Due to our work schedules we used the camper sporadically, but we enjoyed it immensely when we did get to use it.

The camper was situated on a spit of land between the Pamlico Sound and the Atlantic Ocean. This was an ideal spot for windsurfing as the wind was strong and consistent and the water was relatively flat. Just what one needed to go fast! The day's choice was easily made when in the early morning I would take Jammer the Springer Spaniel up to the sand dunes to do his business. As he was running around, I would look over to the sound to see if there were white caps on the water. If so, it would be a wind-surfing day; if not, it would be a beach day. Decision made.

We owned the trailer for approximately four years until "the storm of the century," a March storm, raced up the Eastern Seaboard from Florida and flooded the trailer with salt water from the Pamlico Sound. The water hit with such force that the trailer was shifted around on its cinder-block stands, even though it was anchored to the ground. Decks floated away and some were found up in the sand dunes. Farther south on Hatteras Island, homes were lost. A few homes were broken into by people seeking shelter from the rising water.

We were fortunate as our insurance covered our loss. After reverting back to motels for a year, Teri declared that she wanted a house on the Outer Banks, one farther north where there is more protection from the storms.

She wanted to look for a beach house on Colington Island, which is on the eastern end of the Albemarle Sound, directly behind the Wright Memorial on the Outer Banks. Colington Harbour is a canal community and is very boating oriented. It is not as good for windsurfing as Hatteras Island, but life is full of compromises and we would have a "beach house." We bought the house and enjoyed it together until August 1997.

Shortly after Teri was transferred to the evening shift, a strong rumor circulated throughout the police department that I was to be made the administrative lieutenant for the Uniform Operations Bureau. That would mean day shift with weekends off. I approached my captain and explained the strained conditions in which Teri and I found our schedules to have been for twelve years and that, now, we were finally on evening shift and could at least spend mornings together. I said that it would be cruel to transfer me to a day shift position so soon after Teri making it to evenings at Phillip Morris. Capt. Buck Maddra said that he completely agreed and I never heard another word about the administrative job. I didn't want the job anyway. The only place to be was "on the street."

Nothing stays the same, and a year later Capt. Maddra called me into his office to prepare me for an upcoming change in my life. I was being transferred to Support Services, out of operations, and basically to a Monday through Friday day job.

"What have I done wrong to be moved out of operations?" I plaintively asked.

"Absolutely nothing," Buck said. "You are needed over there. Sometimes things aren't as they seem."

Intellectually I believed him, but, emotionally I was stunned. I had served a year and a half in the crime prevention unit as a sergeant and now I would be the unit commander. The previous experience would serve me well, and the department too. This, of course, ended the time Teri and I had together in the mornings.

Upon assuming command of the unit, I found that I had some really good people working there but that they needed some attention. They had great ideas, but needed someone to champion those ideas for them. Within one year of supporting the ideas of my subordinates, the unit had received several state and national awards and recognition. Things were going well professionally.

CHAPTER 27
PROMOTION TO POLICE CAPTAIN

AT ABOUT THE YEAR-AND-A-HALF MARK, another promotional process was initiated. This time I was vying for captain, which had been my ultimate goal when I entered the department. Once again the dreaded reading list and written exam raised their ugly heads. If the candidate were to get beyond those obstacles, then the ultimate test would be the oral panel, comprised of county officials, police managers from other surrounding departments, and police managers from within. A question to which the candidate had 20 minutes to write an answer comprised a major piece of the interview. Yes, write a response, right down my alley. I have always been better at thinking things through before responding. Great! The panel made its recommendation to the chief of police, who made the ultimate decision.

Time moves slowly when candidates are awaiting the outcome of a promotional process. Always, a few are happy with the outcome and many are not. A couple of weeks after the interview process, Chief Joseph E. Pittman, Jr. called me into his office and told me that he was promoting me to the rank of police captain and that I would stay in support services as the division commander. He said that a lot of work needed to be done in that area and that he expected me to get it done. "Yes sir!" My head was spinning when I left the chief's office. I was floating on air; I had just won Olympic gold!

Little did I know that the position of division commander would be the most challenging and difficult assignment in the department. The year and a half in support services found me managing the crime-prevention unit, school resource officers, school crossing guards, the police property room, and county animal control. Any of those functions could bite you at any time, but the property room and animal control were problems waiting to happen. At any given time some demon could raise its head, particularly at animal control. My boss at the time, Louis Moore, was a wonderful man and great friend who was the civilian equivalent to police major, a bureau commander.

One day Lou and I had driven to animal control to inspect the facility. As we were walking back to the car, Lou turned to me and asked, "Dave, in your wildest dreams did you ever expect to be in charge of the pound?" "No, Lou, I did not," was my response. Across the board, I found myself dealing with personnel issues, in all areas of my command. By and large, I had great people, but things do happen, professionally and on the home front. I was quickly learning that along with the paperwork, personnel matters rank high on the list of things to be done by managers.

The Chesterfield County Animal Control Unit was a typical pound-type installation with the responsibility of gathering up stray domestic animals and housing them until they could be adopted out or until their time ran out and they had to be euthanized. Unfortunately, many animals met the fate of euthanasia.

The kennel master had the dual responsibility of caring for the animals and the termination process. What a terrible thing to have to do, over and over again. The animal-control employees were all very good people, but they were stressed to the max. Not only did they have their jobs to manage, but they had to do it under the scrutiny of a citizen animal rights group. The activists may have been well intentioned, but they expected and demanded "the moon." Nothing less, in their eyes, was acceptable.

In meeting with police management, one of the activists stated that the department should be euthanizing via lethal injection and that the employee administering the injection should hold the animal in his lap, cradling the animal to comfort it before administering the killing injection. This should be done for each and every animal. The unit was "putting down" approximately sixty animals every ten days. I can only imagine the effects that the activist's demand would have had on our employees. It was not going to happen.

We did get numerous complaints about animal control, mostly from the activist group but also from ordinary citizens. Some complaints were warranted. Of course, the chief of police heard about all of the complaints, not just the warranted ones. On one occasion the unit allowed a quarantined dog to escape. Obviously, this was bad. The dog was ultimately re-captured, a day later, but the damage was done.

A week or two later, the chief's staff was sequestered for a one day "retreat." During one of the 10-minute breaks, we were gathered in the break room, taking the opportunity to get a cup of coffee or a soft drink and maybe a snack to tide us over until lunch. Col. Pittman, the chief of police, had been talking with several staff members when he spied me and beckoned me over as the others dispersed. As I got close, the chief leaned in toward me, about one foot from my face. With a forced smile, similar to a grimace, he said in a low and very controlled voice, "Hope, if you don't get animal control squared away, I'm gonna cut your nuts out."

I instantly believed him and a vision flashed before me of Buck Maddra and one or two others holding me down while the chief cut away with a big pocket knife. I gulped and responded, "Yes sir!" Believe me when I say there were no further complaints at animal control. I am a firm believer in pain compliance, and the chief had reached my threshold without ever touching me. His concern became my concern. It was already, but now it had my utmost attention, above all else.

My next professional move was to the position of South District Division Commander, Uniformed Operations Bureau, where I commanded over half of the two hundred plus uniformed officers of the police department. This included the three south district shifts, the K-9 squad, marine patrol, and the traffic squad/crash team. Obviously, there was a learning curve involved. My time was divided between numerous meetings, volumes of paperwork, response to major incidents in the south district, and, of course, personnel matters. Though I found this assignment to be the most stressful position I had yet served, it was rewarding.

At about the time that I took this assignment, Chief Pittman, the only chief under whom I had served, retired from the department. A nationwide search was conducted to find Chief Pittman's replacement.

We, of course hoped that someone from within the department would be promoted to chief of police. This was a stressful time within the organization as rumors flew, and the politics were rampant.

Ultimately, the new man was selected from outside and was the highly credentialed Col. Carl R. Baker. After settling in for a couple of months, Col. Baker appointed Dennis McDonald as his deputy chief of police. Dennis had been the insider with the best chance of becoming chief of police had Baker not been selected. The two turned out to be an excellent team in the office of the chief. For about the first six months of Col. Baker's reign, the learning curve for his staff was steep and to a lesser degree for the entire department. I was now a part of his staff.

Time moved on and one morning Col. Baker stopped by my office and said that he needed to see me, but not right then as he was en route to a meeting. I wondered what he wanted.

Two hours later, he stopped by again and said, "I still need to see you, but I can't right now. Tell you what, Dennis, Jim (Major Jim Bourque, Criminal Investigations Bureau commander who retired as a deputy chief of police), and I are going to lunch. Can you go with us, and you can ride with me and we will talk on the way?"

It was more of a command than a question.

"Yes sir, I can go," I said.

"Good," he said, "I'll call you when I'm ready."

As the colonel left, I was thinking, "What is up?"

At about 11:35 Col. Baker called and I met him at his office. We strolled through his outer office and past the secretarial pool and out the door to his car. The colonel always drove.

En route to lunch Col. Baker explained the purpose of our meeting.

"Dave, you know that I have been wanting to create a new bureau within the department," he said.

"Yes sir," I replied.

"Well, I'm going to do that (now I knew that the bureau commander is a police major, not a captain like me; was I about to be promoted?) and I am putting Steve Davis there as the bureau commander."

Now I knew what was coming next; I was going to get Steve's old job, which is a major's position, but something didn't sound right in the colonel's voice.

"Dave, I'm transferring you to the Office of Professional Standards (internal affairs), but I could not create another major's slot. Steve is taking his with him to the new bureau, so you will be the commander of the Office of Professional Standards, but at the rank of captain. How do you feel about that? Don't worry; you will be a major one day."

How did I feel about that? I was going to the most hated position in the department and was not getting the commensurate rank. "Colonel, you know that I will be happy to serve anywhere that you need me."

We met the others for lunch and of course they already knew the score. As we were eating and the group was chit chatting, I was in a daze and my ears were roaring. "Damn, my life is upside down," I was thinking. Lt .Col. Dennis McDonald volunteered that he and Col. Baker had agreed that they needed someone in O.P.S. who could write, as the department was seeking accreditation. They said they knew I would give internal affairs its due.

CHAPTER 28
LIFE TURNED UPSIDE DOWN

SHORTLY AFTER ASSUMING COMMAND of O.P.S., affectionately known as "oops," I took a three- or four-day sailing trip with my pal Dave Enochs. Teri and I had virtually no time off together, and it had been that way for a while. Before the trip I asked her repeatedly if she was sure that she would have to work mandatory overtime on the weekend in question. She assured me that there was no chance that she would be able to have the weekend off. I said that even if she were to find out differently at the last minute, please let me know and Dave and I would go sailing some other time.

Dave and I had our usual great sailing adventure, with the last day, a Sunday, being unbearably hot, just the way we liked it. The added benefit of the heat was that for the first time ever I managed to run over two crab pots simultaneously. The boat immediately slowed to 2 knots, and instantly a pod of dolphins surfaced off our stern, appearing to have a hearty laugh at our expense.

Dave volunteered to dive overboard to free the pots. We were a couple of miles out in the Chesapeake Bay and, of course, the wind was finally picking up. We tethered Dave to a line so that he could not drift away from the boat and we talked about not getting tangled in the line. Dave was a lifeguard during his high school days and he still possessed a high degree of water skills. After several dives, Dave had us free once again, and we continued our trip back to home port.

After unloading and cleaning the boat, it was a one-and-three-quarter-hour drive back home to Chesterfield County. I was tired when I left the marina and exhausted by the time I got home. Teri's car was in the driveway, but it should have been in the parking lot at Phillip Morris where she was supposed to be working mandatory overtime.

She met me in the driveway, something she had never done in the past. All of my police instincts were telling me that something was wrong.

"Teri, what is wrong?"

"David, we have to talk," she said with determination.

We stepped inside our home and I saw that the dining room set was missing, as was the great room furniture.

"Teri, what is going on, where is our furniture?" I asked.

She led me into the Florida room that we had built several years earlier and sat down.

"David, we can't be married anymore," she said.

At that point we had been married right at twenty years. A very direct statement of her feelings ensued, leaving no room for doubt that she meant what she said. We had seen a marriage counselor several times earlier in the summer and I thought that we were making good progress. I guess I was wrong.

I had lost my mother to cancer seven years before, and Dad had passed away the previous September after a very difficult time. This was really the last straw; it was as though Teri had reached inside my chest and pulled my heart out. Really. Neither of us was happy, and Teri finally did something about it, but I was devastated at the time. Of course, the emotions run rampant at a time like that – a sense of great loss, betrayal, devastation, anger and guilt for not having done my best are a few that come to mind.

The following morning, Monday, a work day, I was compelled to report my change of marital status to the office of the chief. It was one of the most difficult things that I had ever done. I had to walk in to Dennis McDonald's office, my friend and also the deputy chief of police, and tell him that Teri and I were separated. In the eyes of others, we had one of those perfect marriages. We, as administrators and managers, dealt with the discord of others, but this was my own. Would it hurt me professionally? It certainly could. I swore that I would not cry in front of Dennis, and while it was difficult, I choked it all back. I then had to tell my subordinates, since I didn't want it coming from rumor.

Yes, I had pride and it hurt. My private life was in shambles, and I did not want my professional life to suffer as well. I had seen it happen many times over. I was at that point a star in the department and did not want that star tarnished nor to stop its ascent.

Ironically, within two weeks I was called into the chief's office where I met with both the chief and deputy chief and was told that rumors were floating around the county government center that I was having several affairs with various secretaries at the same time. Sadly, one of those named was my own secretary, who was a very nice lady with her own family and a person whom I believe would never step outside of her wedding vows. I did not know until long after I retired that she had known about the rumor. It was said to have embarrassed her greatly. I assured my commanders that I was not having an affair with anyone.

Several weeks later, I was called in to the deputy chief's office for a follow up as the rumors had not died. One can easily imagine that some would like to think that the commander of the office of Professional Standards had fallen from grace.

Shortly after that, my office was tasked with investigating some of the most serious internal cases that the department had ever faced. Eight officers were either forced to resign or were terminated for cause as a result of the investigations. Sadly, these had been good officers who stepped out on that slippery slope and began a free fall to disgrace. Two were later re-instated as the civilian appeal board clearly did not understand the case, which actually was very straight-forward. The interviews of the "suspect" officers were conducted in my office by my lead detective. I was present for all of those interviews. It was sad to watch an officer's career collapse in front of me. Only one gave me satisfaction, as he lied and altered documents at every turn of the investigation. He was trying to save his job.

The good thing that can be said is that approximately 92 percent of the complaints that we worked turned out to be unfounded. At the beginning of my assignment to OPS, I told my detectives that I wanted to save the good names of accused police officers when appropriate, but that the facts were of the utmost importance and would lead us where ever they led. My time in OPS. afforded me the opportunity to work directly with the chief and deputy chief and helped me establish an even greater trust in both directions and prepared me for the next move within the department.

CHAPTER 29
NEW BOAT

A MOVE WAS AFOOT in my sailing life as well. I took a day off from work one day early in November 1999, and Jammer the wonder dog and I drove down to Deltaville to visit S/V *Razzle Dazzle*. After checking the status of the boat, Jammer and I both stretched out on the dock, letting the Indian summer sun shine on us. After a brief nap I awoke and asked Jammer if he wanted to go look at a few boats at Norton's Yacht Sales, where the S-2 had been purchased back in 1992. Jammer thought it was a good idea, so off we went.

I had been thinking about a boat that would be better suited for cruising for some time. I wanted something in the 37' range, no more than five years old.

When we arrived at Norton's, about a five-minute drive from the marina, I located Carolyn, the owner. She said that she had something that I might be interested in, a 1998 Hunter 376 sloop that was in very good condition; of course, it should have been, being only one year old. She led me down to the dock where the boat was slipped and left me to scrutinize the boat. I spent well over two hours lifting up cushions and floor boards, opening cabinets, and looking at the engine, sails, hardware, running rigging, standing rigging, and all the nooks and crannies that I could find.

After the inspection Carolyn said that the sister boat would be in the very next day and that it was in even better condition. Would I like to see it? Yes, I would. That evening I drove back home to Chesterfield County and told the new love interest in my life, Hannah, what Jammer and I had found. The following day we drove back down to Deltaville to see the second 376.

It was in better condition, almost perfect with the exception of drill holes on almost every inside bulkhead where the previous owner had hung who knows what. Better condition, of course, translated into more money. After much agonizing and soul searching, I decided that I wanted to make an offer on Hunter 376 #2, S/V *Sapphire*.

Carolyn, an astute business woman, and I came to an agreement with which we could both live. The survey was conducted and a few small things were identified that needed to be corrected, and then she was sea trialed. Carolyn was able to secure for me a very good borrowing rate, and within a couple of weeks I owned a boat new to me.

This was a very exciting time. The Hunter dwarfed my old 30' S-2, was almost brand new, and was a far faster sailor. The first evening on board, sailing friends showed up on Norton's dock and gave us a boat party. Later, we drove to The Galley for supper and more celebrating. A friend bought me a "Dark and Stormy," which I normally don't care for, but that one was great, as was the one after it. I wonder if the name of that drink portended the things to come? I think so.

Hannah insisted that the name *Sapphire* had to go. I agreed but said I liked the name just to get a rise out of her. It worked. I had thought about the name *Summer Breeze*, but another boat in the marina already laid claim to *Summer Breeze*. We tossed around a few ideas, but nothing moved us. Finally one of us said, "What about *Summer Heat?*"

Well, I live for the summertime and the heat that comes with it. We got the name.

The local boat-name painter thought our logo was trailer-park quality and said so, but he agreed to paint it. Tell me what a boat is if it is not a trailer on the water. We had the big red words *Summer Heat* painted on the bow, with a palm tree bending in the wind at one end of the name and a brightly shining sun at the other. People knew that boat when they saw her from a distance.

The winter of 1999–2000 was a long one as I impatiently waited for spring to arrive so that I might sail my new boat. Shortly after the purchase the boat had gone to dry dock for the winter. Spring finally arrived, and *Summer Heat* splashed on the third weekend of March. I always prided myself in being one of the first back in the water after a cold winter. The re-commissioning jobs were taken care of quickly. After all, she was a sail boat and needed to go sailing.

I quickly learned that the fully battened mainsail on that 61.5 foot mast was a bear to hoist. I also learned that I did not know much about sail trim. Whenever my sailing buddy Dave Graf was on board, he would make that boat fly. I would ask, "Dave, how do you trim her to make her go so fast?" He would always respond, "Man, you know how to do it!"

No, I didn't. All he had to do was look at the main and jib, do a little tweaking and the boat would take off, but he couldn't explain it to me. For me, it was all about luck. If I hit upon the right combination, the boat was fast; if not, it was another story. Much later, I regretted not owning that boat when I raced for a few years.

The summer of 2000 was spent in learning the boat, outfitting the boat, sailing the boat, and, of course, working. I planned to retire from the police department in 2002, so I had only a couple of years to get her ready for cruising. A great deal needed to be done, but I could only do so much at a time financially. I bought and installed equipment right up to the last day before the fateful Bahamas trip in November 2002. In fact, Hannah and I were running computer cable the day before we left for Beaufort, N.C., the official starting point of the trip.

Over the two-year period I accomplished quite a bit. The first item I purchased was a ten-foot rigid inflatable boat (RIB) with a 15 hp Mercury outboard. Carolyn was nice enough to buy the RIB and outboard at her discounted price and sell them to me with no mark up (approximately $3,500). Any well-read sailor knows that a good dinghy is of utmost importance when in cruising mode and that a light-weight, inexpensive weekender will not do. A cruiser's dinghy needs large tubes for stability and to keep out as much water as possible. A 15 hp outboard will pop that dinghy up on a plane; nothing less will do.

Weekenders on the Chesapeake often tow their dinghies behind the big boat. That won't do for cruising. I purchased dinghy davits ($1,200) at the U.S. Sailboat Show in Annapolis, Maryland, and had them installed in Deltaville. I toyed with the idea of doing it myself and decided that I didn't want to be the one to drop parts in the creek.

More big-ticket items followed. One of the spreaders, the horizontal piece that holds the shroud (cable) off of the mast and provides tension, was cracked where it attached to the mast. It had to be replaced. While the mast was down, Ken, who is Carolyn's husband and co-owner of Norton's, asked me if I wanted anything installed on the mast as now would be the time to do it. While I wasn't really ready to do it right then, I said yes, let's mount a Raytheon Radar on the mast ($1,500). I purchased the equipment and had Norton's people perform the installation. Fortunately, I had a ten percent discount deal at West Marine due to the purchase of the boat. That helped.

My dad had been a ham radio operator for many years and had tried unsuccessfully to get me to acquire my own amateur license. I wasn't interested for a long time. When I started talking about cruising, before Dad passed away, he said, "If you are going to sail on the ocean you know you need your radio license don't you son?" "Yes, Dad," I said. "I know."

At that time the Icom 710 Marine Single Side Band Radio with amateur frequencies included was the hot radio to have ($1,800). The radio, of course, required an antenna tuner, which is an additional piece ($400) and an antenna. Sailboats generally use an insulated back stay as the antenna, but most Hunter sailboats do not have back stays; therefore, I had a 23' whip antenna installed. Such a radio system requires sufficient ground plane to transmit properly, thus, yards of copper tape were run underneath the floor boards and grounded to various seacock through hulls.

Coupled with the Icom 710 was a Pactor modem ($1,000), which would allow e-mails, weather, and faxes to be transmitted to the laptop computer from the radio. For navigation, I had a Furuno 300 GPS (global positioning system) unit installed at the navigation station. It was interfaced with the laptop computer, for which I purchased navigational software ($300). It was also interfaced with the autopilot, which fortunately, was on the boat when I bought it.

One week before the Bahamas trip, Hannah and I were once again visiting the Annapolis boat show, where we found an interactive remote computer screen that could be mounted at the helm and was supposedly "water resistant" ($2,000). I was sold a plastic cover, just in case. That screen is the reason we were running computer mouse cable the day before we left. Coupled pieces of 15' cable did not provide enough signal strength to make the screen interactive; therefore, I had a cable made to length and we ran it that last day. I wanted a television on board, primarily for local weather, so I purchased a 13" color 12 volt TV. There was no place to mount it, so I had Norton's custom-build a teak shelf to house the TV. That was $800, but the craftsman did such a wonderful job that the finished product looked as though it came from the Hunter factory installed when the boat was built.

Safety items included the following: a 406 EPIRB (emergency position reporting beacon) with built in GPS ($1,200); Winslow six-man offshore inflatable lifeboat with pedestal ($4,200); man overboard pole ($138); life sling ($160), throw rope ($50), jacklines ($100), tethers ($90 x 4); inflatable personal flotation devices ($150 x 2); type one pfds ($50x4); foul-weather gear ($150 x 2); personal strobe lights ($60 x 4); radar reflector ($60); SOLAS grade flare kit ($229); sea anchor ($800); ditch bag ($50) with emergency rations and room for personal documents; flashlights (various prices); Remington 870 marinized 12-gauge shotgun ($700); .45 caliber handgun ($160, 1973 vintage); and an extensive first aid kit ($50). I am sure that I have forgotten a few items. Did I mention emergency beer? Actually, no drinking while sailing.

I did not include the labor costs in this summary, but I assure you that it was extensive.

CHAPTER 30
A GOOD PRACTICE RUN FOR THINGS TO COME

OVER THOSE TWO YEARS I sailed *Summer Heat* every chance I got. I preferred staying out in the Chesapeake Bay, doing as much destination sailing as possible and experiencing whatever came along. On one particular occasion Dave Enochs, Dave Graf, and I took her out for a four-day trip up the bay. We had visited Solomons, Maryland, a long daysail from Deltaville that could be broken up into two short daytrips if needed. We did our usual foot tour of Solomon's Island, visiting our favorite watering holes and Boomerang's Rib place for supper.

The following morning the weather had deteriorated significantly, with the wind at 20 to 25 knots from the southeast and a steady rain. We had voted Dave Enochs to be the chief mate, and he and I were all for staying in Solomons for another day, but the third Dave needed to get back to Deltaville so that he could go to work on Monday.

With some reservations, we pulled out of our comfortable slip and headed out into the remnants of a thunderstorm. As we left the protection of Solomon's Island and entered the Patuxent River, we encountered significant wave action. Since a commercial fishing boat had just met us, I assumed that the waves were a result of his passing. In my somewhat sleepy brain it took a few minutes for it to register with me that the waves had not diminished after clearing the fishing boat's wake. Hmm. I asked the crew if anyone wanted to turn around, but Dave Graf wanted to continue and the chief mate was noncommittal.

Thinking that once we entered the bay the wind would be less on the nose and hopefully we could sail close hauled, I agreed to continue. The weather wasn't dangerous, just very uncomfortable. One must sail/motor far out into the bay in order to avoid the shoal on the south side of the Patuxent. The wind was still on our nose, and the waves were pounding *Summer Heat*. Again I hoped that once we made the turn toward the south, we would be able to sail and not have to pound into the waves. That was not to be. When we made the turn it was readily apparent that we would be motor sailing all day, a very long day at that.

The mainsail was fairly easy to reef. With the reefing lines leading into the cockpit, theoretically, one did not have to leave the safety of the cockpit to initiate a reef. The genoa was on a furler and also simple to reef. We lowered the main to the first reef point and furled the genoa in about one-third of the way. We were still sailing almost directly into the wind and waves, off the wind just enough to keep shape in the sails.

While this was a summer day, we were cold. The wind was 20 to 25 knots and the rain was blowing sideways. Dave Graf did not have proper foul-weather gear with him and was wearing shorts. Dave liked to sail *Summer Heat* and had been at the helm for a couple of hours. Dave Enochs was standing beside him at the helm, but was wearing good foul-weather gear. I had my foulies on and was sitting in the companionway, facing aft. I was well protected by the companionway and the dodger. I happened to look down at Dave Graf's sandaled feet and saw that they were purple. I asked, "Dave, are you cold?" and he replied, "Yes, a little." I asked if he would like some coffee and he replied that he would. This would be problematic as the boat was really getting bounced around and the propane gas tank was located in the swim platform lazarette. This would require someone to step outside of the life lines and climb down onto the swim platform and open the locker to turn on the gas valve. My boat, my job.

The chief mate recognized the danger of this exercise and spoke up, "No one needs coffee!"

I assured him that I would hold on tightly and not fall in. Who was I trying to convince, him or me? I said, "Keep a close eye on me," as I went for it.

First I unsnapped the lifeline, then got a death grip on the stanchion and cautiously stepped down on to the swim platform. The tricky part would be to lift up the heavy locker top, which swings up at an awkward angle. I accomplished this and bent down to turn on the gas while still holding onto the stanchion. I think I stretched my arm length a little that day. I then reversed the procedure and climbed back up to the safety of the cockpit.

The next challenge was to actually heat the water on the stove as I did not have a kettle and had to use a pan while holding on in the huge washing machine which was my boat. The water finally heated and I observed that the water poured out at a 45 degree angle to the attitude of the boat. Weird. Both Daves were very glad to have the hot coffee, and I think that Dave Graf hugged his for a while before drinking it.

The trip from Solomons Island to Deltaville is approximately 60 nautical miles, and it was apparent that slamming into the four-foot-plus seas as we were, we would not make anything close to sixty miles in the daylight. I had no interest in finishing the trip in the dark, particularly under the current conditions. My thought was to try to make the Great Wicomico River, about 25 nautical miles closer than Deltaville.

We agreed to tack across the bay for a while to see if we could get a better angle on the wind. After sailing for a half-hour in the wrong direction, we tacked *Summer Heat* back over and discovered that our efforts had been to no avail. We continued to motor sail on in the general direction of Smith Point Light House and eventually the Great Wicomico.

As we approached the mouth of the Potomac River from the north, the waves increased in size and frequency; also, they were becoming quite confused, coming seemingly from all directions. I had always heard that the Potomac could get to be really a rough place, but I had never experienced it as all of my crossings had been benign. This one was different.

The time was now 1530, or 3:30 PM, and I doubted seriously that we could make the anchorage in the Great Wicomico before dark. We just could not make much headway against the wind and waves. I went down below to the chart table to consult the Chesapeake Bay Chart Book and investigate where we could go that would be closer. It was at least fifteen nautical miles across the mouth of the Potomac to the Great Wicomico, and several more nautical miles to the anchorage.

The interior of the boat was even more like the inside of a washing machine than it had been earlier in the day. I gathered up the chartbook, a notepad, and a pen and secured myself as best I could at the navigation table and poured over the charts. I found the Coan River several nautical miles up the Potomac, on the south side of the river. I had never been there before, but the location looked good to me. It appeared to be a straight-forward entrance with one 90 degree left turn after the entrance. The entrance was wide and deep enough, which was just what I wanted to see right about then. It was time to get secured for the night.

Now I had to plot a course into the mouth of the Potomac with a short ride up the river to the Coan and then the route in to the anchorage. There was so much motion on the boat that I could barely read the coordinates on the chart, much less transpose them onto my notepad, but that is what I had to do. I slowly and deliberately created my route on the chart, transferring the coordinates for each of five waypoints onto the notepad while keeping myself wedged in the seat. I read each coordinate three times before writing it on the pad. After entering the sets of coordinates, I checked them individually three times to see that I had written them down correctly. I placed the sheet of notepad paper in a Ziploc bag and climbed up the companionway to the cockpit.

The maelstrom in the cockpit was continuing as I returned. The next step was to transfer the coordinates from the pad on to the GPS (global position system), which would provide the waypoints to our home for the night. I did not have a chart plotter at the time, just the GPS and the chartbook.

The GPS was mounted on the pedestal directly in front of the steering wheel. The only way to accomplish the task was to reach through the wheel to punch in the numbers. In calm conditions, that would not have been a problem, but with the huge waves and the strong wind, Dave Graf was fighting the wheel continuously. The spokes were moving back and forth with regularity. I would reach through, punch in a few numbers, and jerk my arm out of the way. To complicate matters Dave needed to stand in the same place in which I was standing. Eventually, I entered all of the coordinates and checked them three times each. Now we could begin our trek into the Potomac and to the Coan.

We were now getting shoved around dramatically. The boat was all over the place. The time had come to stow the sails. The genoa would furl onto its extrusion, but the main would be another matter. Someone would have to go forward on deck to secure the main. Dave Enochs, again thinking about our safety, said, "What about the jacklines, aren't you going to deploy them?" Graf and I responded in unison, "It's too late now; we will just have to do it without jacklines." My boat, I was going forward. Dave Graf owned his own boat and said he would go with me. We crept forward, Dave Graf on the starboard and I was on port, holding on to lifelines and grab rails as we went.

The chief mate's job was to point the boat directly into the wind and hold her there until Graf and I could get the main down and secure the sail to the boom with four sail ties. Again, this would be an easy job in calm conditions. As I approached the mast a large wave struck the port side of the bow, sending me across the bow and around the mast.

Fortunately, I had one hand wrapped around an inner "diamond" shroud and was able to hang on. That shroud felt very small in my hand as I flew around the mast. Dave Graf's body stopped my movement as I slammed into him on the starboard side of the boat. Wow, that was close.

I regained my composure and returned to the port side of the mast. We dropped the mainsail and began to collect the sail on top of the boom while holding onto whatever we could with one hand each. Dave had to let go of his hand hold to accomplish a task so I reached over the boom and grabbed the back of his personal flotation device. As he squatted low to the deck he yelled above the noise of the wind and waves, "Something's got me!" I said, "That's me, I've got you, you are OK."

Dave Enochs did a great job of controlling the boat, and we finished the job of securing the main then quickly moved back to the safety of the cockpit. That cockpit felt pretty good after being out in the wild and wooly of the foredeck.

The next issue was to get us to the Coan and then to the anchorage. I took the helm, consulting the way points that I had entered in the GPS as well as checking the chart. Shortly, we approached the entrance to the Coan River and it looked straight forward. As we entered the Coan the wave action decreased dramatically and I thought that I could relax a little. Not to be.

Upon finding the left turn that we needed to make to get to the anchorage, it appeared that the water was shallow all the way across the creek. I checked my waypoint and the chart, and yes, we were in the correct location. The shallow-looking water must have been sand blowing across the entrance of the creek due to the high wind. We had to go through there. Everything said that there was water. I drove *Summer Heat* past the sandy area and it was just that, sand in the water, no problem.

Next we approached red and green marks, leading us to our destination. One problem, though: the markers appeared to be ninety degrees out of sync to what was on the chart.

My nerves were beginning to fray and I said that I needed to consult the chart again and asked Dave Enochs to take the helm. I had him turn the boat around and retrace our progress until I sorted out the differences between what my eyes told me and what the chart said. "Well, we have to go through there," I mused.

I asked Dave Graf to go forward in the hopes that he might somehow see shallow water if we were wrong. That was a ridiculous idea, but I had to try. Enochs stayed on the helm and I was glued to the chart and GPS. As we approached the two markers that seemed to be 90 degrees out of orientation, Graf yelled back to us to slow down. The helmsman needed to make the right-hand turn between the marks, while keeping enough way on to control the boat in the heavy wind. I said to Enochs, "Don't you dare slow down, just make your turn and keep going."

As the old adage goes, never rely on only one source of navigation. The information on the chart was 90 degrees out of kilter to what our eyes told us. I chose to believe my eyes. Dave motored us through the serpentine, and a short distance up ahead was the anchorage. I took the helm and pulled in close to the windward shore, which was marshland and provided little protection from the wind, but we were totally protected from waves. I had Dave Graf deploy a seven-to-one ratio of scope on the anchor rode and then a little more. I slowly backed down on the anchor and waited for the tachometer to read 2000 rpm. I then sat there at 2000 rpm for a minute, letting that anchor dig in to the bottom.

After monitoring the boat for a few minutes, the entire crew went below for a much needed rest and some warmth. I knew that the crew would want a beer and probably many more than one, but I was very surprised when everyone stopped after only one beer apiece. We were that tired. Tired or not, we needed something to eat. I rummaged through the galley lockers looking for easy dishes to prepare as it was still too windy to cook on the grill. With much effort, I opened a couple of canned vegetables and cooked a meat dish on the stove top. Dave Graf exclaimed, "Look, he still has the energy to cook all of that by himself!" It was more the case that we needed food in us and someone had to do it.

Shortly after supper and the requisite clean up, we all went to bed. I wish that I could say that I slept like a rock, but the williwaws blew most of the night, causing the mast and the entire boat to shudder with each passing blast. The anchor held tight and we were secure for the night.

We left early the next morning and sailed to Indian Creek on Fleets Bay, where we dropped off Dave Graf at his truck. The wind was stiff when we left the Coan and stayed up while we sailed to Indian Creek. After dropping off Dave Graf, Dave Enochs and I turned *Summer Heat* back out toward the bay and had one of the best sails ever, as the wind had diminished just enough to give us a great ride. Farther south on the bay, where the wind had not lessened; several boats issued distress calls that day. That particular trip helped prepare Dave Graf and me for some of what we would face in the later ultimate sailing test.

The one thing I've learned for sure about sailing is that keeping a schedule will get you into trouble. On another sailing adventure, Dave Enochs and I sailed north on the Chesapeake, and our stop before heading home and back to work on Monday was to be Solomons Island, Maryland. We always had a great time in Solomons, with all the sailboats and power boats to admire, the village to peruse, and, of course, the watering holes and good eateries to visit.

Sunday morning we awoke before first light as we needed to sail for approximately 60 nautical miles back to Deltaville in order to get to work on the following day. A lightning storm was passing overhead as we first stirred. I told Dave, "Let's let that thing pass before we leave the slip," and he wholeheartedly agreed. The storm finally passed and we got underway, though the marine weather forecast was a bit iffy. It did not sound awful, and we needed to go.

We pulled out of the creek into the Patuxent River and then into the Chesapeake Bay, headed for home. For a number of miles we were fine, enjoying the day and the sailing. Then a weather alert came across the marine VHF radio: "a train of thunderstorms" was expected to pass directly down the Potomac River eastward into the bay and on to the Atlantic Ocean. Hmm, right in our path.

There's no way to steer around a train of storms, they just keep on coming. I elected to slow down and let the storms pass in front of us. But leaving late and slowing down for storms was not going to help our forward progress. We did slow down, and I turned on the radar to see if we could detect the impending weather. Sure enough, we could see on the radar screen that the blob was approaching. It soon looked like Pac Man coming to get us as the black area on the screen got larger and larger. Yikes! We picked up a little breeze from the storm and an insignificant amount of rain, but the storm did pass in front of us.

Seeing a break in the weather, I fired up the engine and motor sailed toward home, which was still a long way off. A second weather alert was announced. This time the storms passed behind us and we escaped unscathed. More miles went by, and now it was mid-afternoon and the third severe thunderstorm announcement came across the radio. This time the area of Fleets Bay was the target. This was bad, bad, bad, as we were at the north end of Fleets Bay and heading south, directly across Fleets Bay to the Rappahannock River and home.

I again turned on the radar. At first, Pac Man was small and taking up just a small part of the screen.

"Maybe it will pass behind us; it looks that way," I said pleadingly. The sky to our southwest was darkening quickly. "Uh, it's moving toward us but maybe behind us."

As time wore on, Pac Man was encroaching on more and more of the radar screen, and the sky was saying the same thing. The storm was moving not just east; it had some northing in it as well. It was going to get us.

I went down below and retrieved two inflatable life vests and brought them up on deck. I put one on, and Dave just looked at the other one. I said, "You better put that on!" Dave looked at me as though I had grown an extra head, but he decided that he should humor me and put the vest on. Within a few minutes the sky turned quite dark, and I said "Hold on, here it comes."

I gripped the wheel, waiting for the blast to hit us and wondering just how far the boat would heel even though we had stowed the sails. Strangely, nothing happened, other than the sky got very dark very quickly and then it passed over. The experience was extremely melodramatic.

Within minutes the VHF cracked to life with boats calling in maydays and requests for assistance. Literally just a few miles away, three waterspouts had crossed the Rappahannock River in the area of Carter's Creek. Had it not been for our earlier delays, we most likely would have reached the Rappahannock in time to encounter the spouts. Several boats experienced heavy damage from these spouts. We motored into Broad Creek, home port, not knowing of the severity of the mayhem. Sometimes we were just lucky.

CHAPTER 31
PROMOTION TO POLICE MAJOR

BACK AT THE CHESTERFIELD COUNTY POLICE DEPARTMENT, another promotional process was in progress. This time there would be no written test for me, as the position of police major was an appointment by the chief of police. I was called to the chief's conference room where I met with Col. Carl R. Baker and Lt. Col. Dennis G. McDonald for a rather informal interview. Dennis and I were academy mates and had been friends and worked together either directly or indirectly for the past 23 years. For the past year and a half, I worked directly for both gentlemen in my role as the commander of the Office of Professional Standards. They clearly knew who they would be getting if they chose me for the job, but they still needed to conduct an interview and there were other very viable candidates to consider.

When a position opens near the top of the chain of command, a ripple effect runs down through the department, impacting all in the chain and those in line positions who want to make a professional move. Thus, the process takes at least a month to accomplish, with resumes, evaluations, testing, selection panels, and the chief's final decision-making process. Time crept by for all who were vying for the various positions. Daily rumors, of course, flew as to who was getting promoted and who would be assigned where. How would that impact the rest of us?

Finally, I was summonsed to Col. Baker's office, almost a daily occurrence in my current assignment, and Lt. Col. McDonald was present also. There was nothing unusual about that, as the two met numerous times daily. The meeting moved quickly with Col. Baker telling me that he was promoting me to the position of major and that I would be commanding the Uniformed Operations Bureau. Wow! The two stood and shook my hand and then we talked about expectations. Later, I floated out of the office, trying my best to suppress a really big grin. This was my dream job, which I hoped would not turn into a nightmare.

My very good friend and professional associate, at the time Major Jim Bourque, had told me when I was promoted to captain that I had no idea of the amount of power that I would have. He was right; the captain's level did wield power. I experienced real power, however, when I assumed the role of Police Inspector, Commander of the Office of Professional Standards. That power was substantial and had the weight of the office of the chief of police directly behind it.

While I did not want it, fear was a very real part of the equation when in internal affairs. I was careful not to scare people as I walked down the halls of the police department. I could clearly see people shrink when they saw me coming. The power associated with the police major's position was not like that, although the power was nearly absolute as only the Office of the Chief was higher. I tried to be judicial with my authority and not wield a heavy hand. I hope that I was successful.

The Uniformed Operations Bureau consisted of 250 sworn positions and several civilian positions. Under the major's command were two district captains, nine lieutenants, forty-five sergeants, and two hundred plus patrol officers. That included six patrol shifts, three in the north district and three in the south district, the Special Operations unit with the crash team (serious traffic accident investigation and selective traffic enforcement), the marine patrol, the K-9 Squad, Street Drug Unit, the Larceny from Auto Task Force, and the regional air unit.

Much of my work was administrative, participating in the various weekly intra department meetings as well as county-wide meetings and regional meetings. Budget work was something I always looked forward to – about as much as visiting the dentist. What was generally enjoyable were the meetings with my own staff and the direct contact with the street police officers. I still responded to major incidents when possible, to "wave the flag" and demonstrate that street-level activity is important to upper management. We in management lived vicariously through the radio traffic of our subordinates out on the street. It was always a great feeling when one or a number of our people made a significant arrest.

Upper management played a significant role in certain cases, such as hostage situations, S.W.A.T. callouts, homicide, lost children or elderly people, or any critical event. Ultimately, there was still police work to be accomplished, not just administrative detail. At that time, Major Jim Bourque (retired as deputy chief of police) commanded the Criminal Investigations Bureau, which included all criminal investigations, both suit and tie and covert. Oftentimes, Jim and I would be summoned to the chief's office where Col. Baker, Lt. Col. McDonald, Major Bourque, and I would discuss whatever operational issue was at hand. The two chiefs valued our input and truly listened to our ideas or thoughts on the given situation. Of course, the ultimate decision rested with Col. Baker, the Chief of Police.

These were my three best years with the Chesterfield County Police Department. In the last six months of my employment I was involved in just about every serious case imaginable to include a barricaded suspect with a hostage, homicide, police vehicular pursuit with injury, and a bank robbery, to name a few. It was as though the forces were saying "drink this up because it will be your last."

It was with great deliberation and some consternation that I decided to retire so that I could go sailing. After all, I had worked toward the top for my entire career and as the Uniformed Operations Bureau Commander had found the position that was my perfect fit. Now I was considering giving it up after only three years. I was also giving up an identity, that of being part of a great organization, one in which I had grown up in professionally. I was giving up being a Chesterfield County Police Officer. That is a lot.

I wanted to "go sailing," and I believed that I needed to be young enough and fit enough to withstand the demands that sailing would require. I still believe that the body needs to learn what is required of it day in and day out to manage a sailboat; then, as one ages, the body will remember how to respond. The brain is the same way. Some sailing procedures need to be rote. In some situations there is not time to think about what to do next; one just has the time to react. So I retired.

Tradition held that people with rank retired with a formal retirement party held in the retiree's honor. When a line employee retired, generally his/her squad, shift, or unit would host a party with all being invited. Over the past several years, several ranking officers had retired and elected not to have the traditional party, but to have a reception for a couple of hours in the afternoon that anyone could attend. Not me; I wanted to have the party.

To set up the function requires a great deal of work on someone's part, and my administrative lieutenant, Ralf Bartley, volunteered for the job. This involves finding an establishment large enough to hold the party and a staff willing to host it. Invitations go out to all of county government and to the regional police departments. Since I served on the chief's staff, that group would chip in and find an appropriate gift. Hannah, my love interest at the time, contacted Ralf and said that she would like to help with the planning. Unknown to me, they met and planned out a fantastic event.

One of Hannah's business endeavors was that she did balloon decorations. On the night of the event I was totally in awe when I walked into the downstairs meeting room of the local Chesterfield Airport. Hannah and Ralf had balloons everywhere – balloon arches, balloon palm trees, a balloon sun and the entire Caribbean-style motif of *Summer Heat*. Hannah had found some of my old police photographs, dating all the way back to my East Carolina Police Department days and had them on display. While there was a keg of beer or two and plenty of other things to drink, I had one draft beer the entire evening. I was having too much fun to bother with drinking. That was a magical, wonderful night. One long-term police department employee said that, by far, it was the best retirement party ever.

CHAPTER 32
RETIRE TO THE BEACH AND OCEAN SAILING

I OFFICIALLY RETIRED on March 1, 2002. I now had the time and freedom to finish getting *Summer Heat* ready to go south for the winter. I had eight months, so I needed to get busy.

The first hurdle was to make the move to the beach house on the Outer Banks. I had sold my Chesterfield County residence six months prior and had been living in an apartment while waiting to retire. While the apartment was nice, both Jammer and I were ready to leave the apartment and get down to the beach.

Interestingly, when I had moved out of my house six months earlier, after the last box left the master bedroom, I sat down and the tears started flowing. I had lived in that house for twenty-two years and many memories were there. Funny, I thought I would leave that house without ever blinking an eye.

Summer Heat was still slipped at Sting Ray Harbor in Deltaville, so after the move to the Outer Banks was completed, I turned my attention to her. I took some of the proceeds from the sale of my house and finished outfitting the boat to be a cruiser. The local electronics technician and I spent many hours together running wires and installing electronics. While it was expensive, I did not mind paying for the tech's expertise and the knowledge that the job was done correctly. The added bonus was that I was at his side and saw what was done and how to do it.

One of the challenging installations was a power anchor windlass. After the installation I found that the anchor well was not deep enough for the chain to fall properly into the locker. Raising the anchor required that as the anchor came up, the chain had to be continuously pushed around with a boat hook so that the chain did not bunch up at the base of the windlass. That was still better than hauling the anchor up by hand.

For some time I had been looking for opportunities to get some ocean sailing under my belt. On three separate occasions I was afforded the opportunity to sail with my good friend Tim Henry and his dad, John, on John's 37 foot Moorings Beneteau sloop, the *Barbara J*, on deliveries up and down the East Coast.

For a number of years John single-handed the boat to Florida and back home to Montauk each fall and spring. While John did not really need the help, I am sure that he was glad to have his son sail with him, and John was gracious enough to allow me to participate. We did some inside (Atlantic Intracoastal Waterway) work, which was instructional, but what I really needed was the ocean experience.

The ocean work consisted of sailing on the outside from Norfolk, Virginia, to Atlantic City, New Jersey, twice. We also made the trip once in the southerly direction. From Norfolk south, John usually stayed on the inside. All three trips were uneventful and consisted of motoring, sailing, and motor sailing. I learned that I had a good inner ear and experienced no problem with seasickness, though I do believe that anyone can get sick under the right conditions. Those trips were my first real experience at night sailing and sailing for more than a day at a time continuously.

In the spring of 2002 I saw an ad in one of my sailing magazines about a Delmarva sailing circumnavigation, which was being sponsored by Nautec Enterprises of Annapolis, Maryland. I had been thinking about that trip anyway and thought this would be the perfect opportunity to sail my own boat around the Delmarva Peninsula.

I contacted the owner of Nautec Enterprises, Capt. Jim Favors, and learned that he and his wife, Margie, would be leading the trip. The opportunity sounded good to me and I signed on. Hannah was eager to go, and we recruited a good sailing friend, Pete Haley, to go with us. Jammer the sailing Springer made the fourth crew member.

Ultimately, approximately twenty-seven sailboats entered the rally. Jim patterned his rally after some of the very successful rallies that go from the U.S. East Coast to the Virgin Islands each winter. The participants of the Delmarva 200 Rally were to meet at a marina mid bay on the Chesapeake Bay, Herrington Harbor South Marina. The weekend was structured with meetings, seminars, boat inspections, and parties. The fleet left Herrington Harbor South Marina at first light on departure day and headed north up the bay. The first day was a long day of motoring as there was no wind at all. Evening found us tied up at the C and D Canal Marina for the night, where we had another unofficial party.

The second day began at first light, motoring up the Chesapeake and Delaware Canal to the Delaware River and bay. As we entered the Delaware River, the wind began to build, but, of course, from dead ahead. When we entered the Delaware Bay, the wind had freshened, and the wind and tide opposed one another, creating big waves. We pounded the length of the bay and approached the North Atlantic Ocean in late afternoon with the wind still up, but beginning to lessen.

Summer Heat was fairly fast under motor, and we were in the bottom portion of the first third of the fleet. The leading boats had reported very rough conditions as they entered the ocean at the mouth of the Delaware Bay. By the time that *Summer Heat* entered the ocean, the waves had subsided substantially, only an hour or two later at the most. As we made the turn south to run down the coast toward Norfolk, we were able to set our sails and sail close hauled. What a great relief to finally turn off the noise maker and do what a sailboat is supposed to do – sail.

Supper time was upon us. Pete, a fantastic amateur Italian chef, had cooked a pot of jambalaya before leaving home and had frozen it in a huge freezer bag. All he had to do was re-heat the stuff in a pot. By then, the wind was 10 to 12 knots and the waves were small, so it was no problem to use the stove. In short order, three bowls of steaming hot jambalaya appeared in the cockpit. The aroma had been wafting up through the companionway for some time, and I was really ready to eat. I knew that it would be good, as I had experienced Pete's culinary endeavors previously.

As I leaned into the task at hand, I noticed that both Pete and Hannah had taken only a few bites of their meal and abruptly stopped. What I learned on that occasion was that only an iron-clad stomach could tolerate the spiciness of jambalaya while sailing on the ocean. I think the sausage did them in, and I am sure that the fire that Pete added did not help matters. I could not help myself; I went back for another half a bowl. Mine stayed down just fine, although there might have been some rumbling around down there. Jammer had no problems cleaning up the remainder of the un-eaten bowls.

The evening and night provided a gentle and quiet sail, but by about 0300 we had to turn on the iron jenny (engine) to keep any speed at all. I learned that night to always have one's route in place ahead of time, although plans can change at any time. Fatigue and even the smallest continued movement contribute to difficulty in concentration when poring over paper or electronic charts. Now would not be the time for sloppy work.

When I awoke from my break, we were experiencing first light of the following day. In two or three more hours we would approach the mouth of the Chesapeake Bay and enter at the northern entrance channel at the Chesapeake Bay Bridge Tunnel. The wind was still light, and we motor-sailed. We saw several of the 27 boats we started with on the horizon. One or two were a little closer to shore or a little farther out. I was excited to be bringing my own sailboat in to the bay from an overnight ocean leg.

We arrived at Salt Ponds Marina in Hampton, Virginia, in the early afternoon. I had sailed into Salt Ponds previously, so the entrance was uneventful, just the way I like it. The marina is directly off of the bay, just inside a little creek with great marshland on the opposite side. The entrance is quite narrow, with a hard left turn immediately after entering the creek. The shallows can be seen on each side of the channel and can be intimidating.

We found our assigned slip and got tied up. Though we were exhausted, we were ready for the trip's-end party to begin.

Much needed showers were the first order of business after pulling three beers from the refrigerator. As we departed the boat for the showers, I looked back at Jammer asleep in the cockpit and wondered if I should have put him down below. No, I thought, he is asleep and will be fine. Plus, I knew he couldn't jump off the boat anyway. At that point in his life, my well-behaved companion and friend was close to thirteen years old.

Of course when we got back, Jammer was nowhere to be seen. He had gone looking for me. Feeling kind of sick, I started down the docks, frantically looking for my dog. A passerby asked if I was looking for a brown and white dog and I said, "Yes." He said that Jammer had gone down the dock in the other direction. I thanked him profusely and started down the dock. When I got to the first turn, there he was, coming toward me. "No more cockpit time for you unattended, Jam."

Nautec Enterprises hosted an official end of the rally party at Salt Ponds Marina. Various prizes were awarded to individual boat captains for such things as "first boat to finish," "last boat to finish," and "largest fish caught." All boats completing the rally received a certificate of participation.

In Capt. Jim Favors' closing statements, he announced that Nautec Enterprises would be conducting a rally to the Bahamas in the late fall of the same year, 2002. The trip was titled "The Bahamas 500 Rally." It would depart Beaufort, North Carolina, and go straight to Marsh Harbor, Abaco, the Bahamas, which was approximately 500 nautical miles away, thus the name of the Bahamas 500 Rally.

Hannah, Jammer, and I were planning to sail to the Bahamas during the same time period, but my plan was to work our way down the Intracoastal Waterway (ICW) to Florida, then hop across to the Bahamas. Jim's proposed trip caught my attention for several reasons. One, we had just completed a successful trip with Jim. Two, my route would take an estimated month to complete, while Jim's rally would be four to five days in the ocean and then we would be at our destination. That meant more time in the Bahamas.

Three, I really wanted the experience of ocean sailing for that length of time. The rally would be organized with numerous boats participating. Some would say that multiple boats increase the safety of all, but I did not believe that to be the case as the boats would be separated as soon as they left Beaufort and the distances would increase with the passage of time. Having said that, there would be benefits to sailing with the flotilla, such as scheduled radio check-ins several times daily. We would have the services of a professional weather router. If a boat did have a serious problem, maybe someone would be near enough to respond. If not, at least advice could be sought over the radio.

Lastly, we would be employing the services of a professional rally leader and could rely on his expertise to get us safely to the Bahamas. My plan would have had us traveling alone but maybe picking up a "buddy boat" in West Palm Beach, Florida, for the crossing.

When Jim finished speaking, I walked to the front of the room and said to him "Sign me up." He stepped back up to the microphone and announced that "Dave Hope and *Summer Heat* just signed up for the Bahamas 500 Rally."

The Delmarva 200 Rally was officially finished, and most of the boats needed to make their way back up the Chesapeake to their respective home ports. Jim Favors led a group back north. Home for *Summer Heat* was still Deltaville, a three-quarter day trip. We decided to take an extra couple of days and lead four or five of the remaining boats to one of our favorite anchorages on the Great Wicomico River, Horn Harbor, directly across the river from the Horn Harbor Marina and Restaurant. It was fun to show one of our favorite spots to these folks from farther up the bay, and it was a great way to wind down from the excitement of the rally.

After the rally it was time to take *Summer Heat* back to Deltaville to finish the outfitting for the upcoming Bahamas trip. Throughout the summer I was making the three-and-a-half-hour trip from the Outer Banks to Deltaville to complete the outfitting. I was tiring of the grind and was ready to take *Summer Heat* home to the Outer Banks and to her own private slip behind the house.

Before that could be accomplished, I needed to dredge out the slip area to have enough depth for the five-foot draft of *Summer Heat*. This had been accomplished during the previous winter after much research and acquisition of various permits. The job was so small that businesses did not want to be bothered with dragging their dredge to my house in Colington Harbour just to dredge out my little 45'x 20' slip. I finally found a local construction company that brought a backhoe to my yard and scooped several dump-truck loads of sand from my slip. Of course, the back yard was completely torn up from the tracks of the backhoe. It took a couple of years for the lawn to recover.

Finally, it was time to deliver the boat to Colington Harbour. This would be the completion of one of my dreams from the time that Teri and I had purchased the "beach house" back in 1995.

The trip from Deltaville to the Outer Banks can be done in two very long days with a boat the size of *Summer Heat*, a 1998 Hunter 376 sloop, or an easier trip can be made in three days. I had done the trip a couple of times on friends' boats and had a good idea of what to expect. This would have been a warm up for the trip down the ICW to Florida had I not decided to do the rally from Beaufort.

Hannah and I sailed *Summer Heat* from Deltaville to Portsmouth, Virginia, and took a slip at the Tidewater Yacht Center the first day. The second day was busy with negotiating the numerous bridges from Norfolk to the Virginia state line and the locks at Great Bridge,

Virginia. Several bridges are restricted for a couple of hours each morning and each evening during the respective rush hours. Sitting at a bridge for two hours can really interrupt a schedule. Plus, it can be quite challenging to maintain boat control in a narrow channel while dealing with wind and current for two hours. It's far better to leave early enough or wait until after the restricted times to move the boat. I have since learned to make that day's passage on the weekend if at all possible to avoid the weekday restrictions.

The second night was spent at the Coinjock Marina in Coinjock, North Carolina, on the "Virginia Cut," a manmade canal joining the Currituck Sound and the North River. The following and last day would be an easy 26 or so nautical mile trip to Colington. We slept in, not leaving at first light as usual. I planned this last leg to arrive at Colington at approximately 1400 (2 PM).

The North River is a very winding and narrow river, and one must be careful not to cut the bends in the river, running from one marker to the next. Once out of the channel, one could find oneself in literally two feet of water. This stretch is beautifully remote with savannahs stretching as far as one can see, lush green in the summer and golden in the late fall or winter. Blue herons, white egrets, seagulls, and other various sea birds are abundant from the Great Bridge locks all the way to the Albemarle Sound.

The last several miles of the North River widen dramatically and straighten substantially before reaching the Albemarle Sound. This stretch can be sailed, assuming the wind is coming from the correct direction. One must still keep the boat in the channel.

As we approached the Albemarle, we hoisted the heavy, full-battened mainsail and unfurled the jib. We sailed out into the Albemarle Sound and turned east toward home. Tears of joy came to my eyes and I jumped up and down with excitement as my dream was coming true. I said, "Hannah, we are sailing on the Albemarle Sound on my boat, not someone else's." I could not contain my exuberance, nor did I want to.

It was a glorious sail to Colington Harbour and one of accomplishment. The only challenge left was the last one and three quarter miles to the harbor itself. With a little bit of local knowledge from my friend Frank Silver, for whom I had been crewing on races, I knew how to avoid the shallow water to the immediate north of the "channel." Still, I saw a nail-biting one foot of water under the keel, or six feet total. That took some getting used to, but when sailing the sounds of North Carolina shallow water is the norm.

We put *Summer Heat* in her new slip for the first time and welcomed her home. Standing on the deck of my house, I was so proud and happy to see my wonderful boat floating in her own slip. I had never expected to own a boat that nice or that expensive. I knew that I was very fortunate to do so.

The remainder of the summer and most of the fall of 2002 consisted of sailing *Summer Heat* to various destinations around the Outer Banks, finishing the readying of *Summer Heat* for the Bahamas, and racing with Frank Silver on his 44' Bavaria sloop named *Sea Ya*. During October, we began acquiring goods for the six months that we intended to live aboard.

We drove the eighty miles to Chesapeake, Virginia, in order to shop at one of the discount stores for canned goods, medical supplies, batteries to fit all sorts of lights and devices, etc. We purchased cases of green beans, black-eyed peas, canned turkey, canned chicken, pasta, dried milk, and whatever else that we could find that was agreeable to our taste buds and diets. Various over-the-counter medicines such as pain relievers, cold remedies, anti-gas tablets, and anti-diarrhea pills made it into our basket. The selection of canned goods was not comprehensive enough to satisfy one's palate for six months, and upon our return to the Outer Banks, we shopped at the local grocery store to fill out our remaining needs. We purchased more canned goods and fresh meats and re-packaged and froze the meat at home so it would be ready to be placed in the boat's freezer at the last minute. We made numerous trips to West Marine and the NAPA store for fuel filters, oil filters, fan belts, and engine oil, and bought toilet paper from West Marine in a large enough quantity to get a discount.

We stored the canned goods in the spare bedroom, living room, and wherever we could find places until we were ready to move them to the boat. Hannah went to the local Kmart and found plastic bins of various sizes to be fitted into the nooks and crannies of *Summer Heat*. She found a large plastic bin that made a good clothes closet, but we had no place to put it. Out came the rather useless cushioned seat from the master stateroom and the plastic bin was bolted down in its place.

As the departure date approached, we began loading all of the above items on board. This took several days to accomplish as not only did we have to carry six months of supplies onto *Summer Heat*, but also they had to be stowed. We made an inventory of where all items were stowed. By the time we finished loading the boat, the grass had been worn down from the house to the boat and a trail had been blazed. The boat's waterline could barely be seen due to the added weight on board.

As stated earlier, as a result of our last-minute trip to the U.S. Sailboat Show in Annapolis, Maryland, we were running computer wire from the navigation station to the binnacle at the helm station on the day before we departed Colington Harbour.

CHAPTER 33
BEGINNING OF THE END

THE DAY FINALLY CAME to depart Colington Harbour and begin the great adventure. All participants of the Bahamas 500 Rally were to rendezvous in Beaufort, North Carolina, on Friday, November 8, 2002. That meant we would have to depart Colington on November 6, as the trip to Beaufort would be two long days of motoring.

We pulled away from home dock, at our back yard, at first light. I was very excited to be underway. On board with me were Hannah and Jammer. My cousin Jeff Akins and good friend and sailing associate Dave Graf were to meet us in Beaufort. Jeff had volunteered himself for the trip.

As we approached the Colington harbor, Frank Silver and his race crew met us on the *Sea Ya* and escorted us up the Albemarle Sound to the Alligator River and then all the way to the beginning of the Alligator/Pungo Canal, some 35 statute miles total.

Upon leaving the dock, I heard *Sea Ya* hail *Summer Heat* on the radio. I replied but received no answer. I replied several more times and still got no answer. I considered taking the time to climb the mast to check the antenna, but on the next transmission, Frank answered. I decided to monitor the radio closely; if there really was a problem, I would deal with it in Beaufort.

As both boats traveled together for the 35 statute miles, there were no further radio problems. I never did know if it was my radio or Frank's, but it wasn't the way I wanted to start the trip.

Near mid-day, the two boats approached the canal and we pulled near to say our goodbyes until the following spring. We were really on our way. We continued down the Alligator/Pungo Canal for twenty miles, heading toward Belhaven, North Carolina, our stop for the night and a total of 75 statute miles from Colington Harbour.

Several options existed for stopping. We could take a slip at Forest View Marina or anchor directly off of town, or we could motor a couple of miles farther to Pungo Creek and anchor there. The cruising guide suggested that holding was not good right off of town, so we continued to Pungo Creek, which turned out to be a beautiful and serene anchorage. A small spit of land protruded from shore, providing the protection we needed for the night. The sun was going down as we dropped and set the anchor. We rushed to lower the dinghy and mount the 15 horsepower outboard on the dinghy's transom so that Jammer could be taken ashore. The last light of day disappeared from the sky as all three of us stretched our legs on the sandy beach. *Summer Heat*'s anchor light led us back to her, and the sky was dark when we climbed back into the dinghy to return to our floating home. We left the dinghy in the water for the following morning's run to the beach for Jammer's chance to "use the bathroom" once again.

Hannah quickly began working on the side dishes for supper while I set up the propane grill and cooked steaks for our first evening's meal of the trip. The chill of the evening was already setting in, and by the time we were ready for bed, it was cold.

The night passed quickly since we needed to depart at first light or a little after, in order to arrive in Beaufort in a timely manner. After taking Jammer to shore and returning to the boat, we raised and stowed the outboard as quickly as possible, followed immediately by the dinghy. The dinghy was stored on dinghy davits and lashed down tightly to avoid chafing the Hypalon body of the dinghy as the boat moved through the water.

The morning started off sunny but cold, and fortunately the temperature warmed throughout the day. We encountered many boats heading south, down the Intracoastal Waterway as were we. This was the first time that I had taken my boat on this portion of the Waterway, but I had been on the Waterway several times previously on the boats of friends. I knew the protocols of Waterway usage and practiced them religiously. The Waterway is infamous for the way a few rude, uncaring boaters conduct themselves when approaching, passing, or being passed by other boats. Guilt falls to power boaters and sailors alike. Fortunately, the vast majority of boaters just want to get along with one another, often offering timely information on hazards up ahead.

For a first-timer, the approaches to Beaufort can be confusing, if not a little intimidating. Resorting to the Cruisers' Guide, I learned that the dredged and commercially used Beaufort Channel was the recommended channel, even though the marina was located on the Gallants Cut Channel. Gallants Cut was allegedly not well marked and boats "often" went aground there. I chose the well-marked and dredged Beaufort Channel, noting that a side channel led directly from the Beaufort Channel to Gallants Cut and the small harbor in which the marina was located. Great.

When I arrived at the side channel, I slowly and deliberately made the turn to port to head into the harbor, perhaps a quarter-mile away. Turning into the side channel I said to Hannah, "This just doesn't look right," and slowed to almost a stop.

The depth sounder read less and less water. Having sailed in the Albemarle Sound, I was accustomed to little water under the keel, but this was getting nerve wracking, quickly. Three feet under the keel (eight feet deep), two feet, then only one foot under the keel. I shifted into reverse, but it was too late. The screen went blank, and the boat stopped its forward motion with a bump. Yes, we were aground.

After working the boat backward and forward, I was able to spin the boat around and head back toward Beaufort Channel and deep water. But what to do now? I knew that I was in the right place, but there was just no water and the markers did not look right.

I hailed the marina on the VHF radio and asked for advice. I was told that the side channel had shoaled in a number of years ago and no longer existed, but that it was still on the charts. Isn't that wonderful? The radio operator suggested that I proceed down Beaufort Channel to the bridge where the water would be deep enough to execute a U-turn and come up the other side of the shallow area; then I could enter the harbor at that point. I followed his advice, although my confidence was a little rattled, and entered the harbor without further incident.

I approached the fuel dock and someone came out to *Summer Heat* and insisted that we throw him a dock line, which he promptly dropped in the water. Never mind that it was a new line and that I would be short one line. Good omens abound!

Friday evening was the official welcoming party to the Bahamas 500 Rally, where we met the crews of the eighteen participating boats and received the first briefing of what was to come over the weekend and on the rally itself. An air of excitement permeated the room, with people talking about their boats, sailing experience, and preparation for the rally. The folks who sat around our table that evening, we tended to socialize with throughout the weekend. Our friends Rankin Tippins and Sandy Hollis of S/V *Heart of Texas* were present also.

Hannah and I were somewhat responsible for Rankin and Sandy participating in the rally. Back during mid-summer, *Summer Heat* was in dry dock at Norton's Yacht Sales in Deltaville, and Hannah and I were performing "grunt" work on the boat – sanding and painting the hull with antifouling bottom paint.

I had been working along for a while and Hannah had disappeared. Ready for a break and curious as to where she could be, I ambled down toward the office and the docks. One of Norton's employees had seen her walking toward the docks. I proceeded down to the far end of the dock where I found Hannah talking to a couple on a Hunter 450 center cockpit sailboat. The female part of the crew was very good looking, so I thought I should be polite and stick around for the conversation.

As it turned out, Rankin and Sandy were from Houston, Texas, and had sailed from Texas to the East Coast. They needed to have some work performed on their boat and found Norton's Yacht Sales, a very reputable Hunter sailboat dealer and known for its customer service. During the conversation, we learned that all of us planned to go to the Bahamas for the winter. Hannah and I told Rankin and Sandy about the Bahamas 500 Rally and that we would be participating. After some consideration, the *Heart of Texas* crew decided to travel with the rally also. We kept in touch over the summer and the fall and were glad to see Rankin and Sandy at the welcoming party.

Saturday and Sunday were filled with boat inspections, planning briefings, weather briefings, seminars, and another get together each evening. An inspection was conducted on each boat to see that the required safety equipment was on board and for a general safety inspection of the boat. A checklist had been devised, and each captain was responsible for the inspection of another captain's boat. If any equipment was missing or not up to standards, a West Marine store was in the local area.

Part of the required safety equipment included a man-overboard pole, a horse shoe life ring, and a life sling. These had also been required on the Delmarva 200 Rally, so I already possessed them. At first blush, I thought that requiring all of these items plus a host of other equipment was excessive, until I realized that the three mentioned items were to be used as a system. Similar items are on my boat today.

Jeff arrived on Saturday and was able to participate in the events of the weekend. Dave Graf was due to arrive on Sunday, but we learned late Saturday that due to weather, we most likely would have to wait until Wednesday morning to depart. The original departure date was Monday. I called Dave Graf and gave him the option of not coming to Beaufort until Tuesday evening. Dave elected to continue working and he planned to arrive Tuesday evening.

At the Sunday evening weather briefing, Jim Favors said that a strong cold front would definitely pass over Beaufort sometime Tuesday Night or Wednesday Morning, and that we would not leave until the front passed. Jim was receiving his information from Commander Weather Service, a private weather routing service that we would use throughout the rally. This was another reason that I had decided to participate in the rally – professional weather routing.

During the weekend, I caught a nasty cold and tried desperately to get rid of it before the Wednesday departure date. I took the usual over-the-counter cold remedies to dry up the sinus passages and stop the sore throat and other symptoms.

Finally Tuesday evening arrived and we had the last briefing before the Wednesday morning departure. Dave Graf had arrived and was at the meeting. The front was still scheduled to pass overhead some time during the night, and we were to depart at 0600 Wednesday morning. Another system was trying to form south of the Bahamas and could potentially pose a problem. Jim said that we would need to "beat feet south as fast as possible" to avoid the new system if it formed.

He further said, "We will be here another week if we do not go now." I will never forget those words. They bothered me at the time and they echoed in my ears throughout the trip. The "beat feet south" phrase became the mantra of the trip, as we heard it at each and every weather briefing once we got underway.

My little inner voice was telling me that it was not a good idea to leave on Wednesday knowing that another system was trying to form south of the Bahamas. Admittedly, I allowed the influence of our professional leader and that of group-think to sway me. All of the other captains must have thought it was OK, as all boats were scheduled to leave Wednesday morning on the rally.

Further flawed thinking involved the fact that most if not all crews had crew members who took vacation to go on this trip. Those folks would not be able to wait another week. *Summer Heat* had two crew members in that situation, and I did not want to send them home without going on the trip. Today, I would send them home without batting an eye. But then, though I did have misgivings about departing on Wednesday morning, I decided that I must be being overly cautious. Let's get out on the water and everything will be fine, I thought.

Most boats had one last party Tuesday evening before the Wednesday morning departure. We certainly did, as Dave Graf had just arrived. This was not a particularly good idea as we did not need to be dehydrated at the beginning of the trip. I was already dehydrated from the cold medicine, but hey, I thought, I'm a trooper; two or three beers won't hurt.

Returning to the boat that evening, we had four people and one dog to get settled in for the night. Personal gear was stowed as best as we could, and we all turned in to get as much sleep as possible. Wednesday morning came very early as we were to depart at 0600. I had secured the boat's shore-power cord and was about to remove one of the dock lines when Rick of S/V *Shanty Irish* approached and said that the departure time had been changed to 1000. Jim Favors had been on the telephone with Commander Weather, who told Jim that the front had not yet passed Beaufort and would pass at around 0900. Commander Weather recommended that we not leave until 1000 when we would catch the backside of the front and get a nice push down the Atlantic. I went back to bed for a while, but sleep at that point was nonexistent.

CHAPTER 34
DEPARTURE

AT 1000 ON NOVEMBER 13, 2002, 18 sailing vessels departed Beaufort harbor and entered the north Atlantic Ocean en route to Marsh Harbor, the Bahamas. The crew of *Summer Heat* was excited to get underway, and I feel certain that all of the other crews were equally excited. We wound our way through the harbor channel and finally out into the Atlantic. We sailed out to the sea buoy before turning south. The wind was blowing at about 20 knots, and *Summer Heat* flew all of her cloth on a broad reach.

We had a great sail for about an hour, and then the situation deteriorated quickly. Suddenly, the wind was at about 30 knots, and *Summer Heat* was overpowered. We needed to reduce sail quickly. Had I fallen off the wind further, the main would have blanketed the jib enough to alleviate much of the wind power and reefing or partially furling the jib would have been easier. I did not opt for that choice; rather, I chose to head up into the wind, gaining control of the boat but not the sails.

Both the mainsail and the jib began flogging violently, and we needed to get the sails under control immediately. We began by partially furling in the jib so that it would be properly reefed for the conditions. Of course, the main was flogging while the crew worked with the jib. After reefing the jib, our attention turned to the flogging mainsail. Only a couple of minutes had passed, but a great deal of flogging had occurred during that time.

Fortunately, the main on *Summer Heat* could be reefed from the cockpit. Theoretically, no crew member would have to climb out of the cockpit and go forward to handle the sail. The reefing lines were rigged to the reefing points of the main, run down the mast and through the boom, all leading to the cockpit and clutches on the cabin top. The main halyard was also led to the cockpit, which meant that the main could be lowered easily while in the safety of the cockpit, not the case when raising the sail.

In fairly short order the main was lowered to the first reefing point and the reefing line drawn tight and locked into the clutch or brake. The main halyard was then re-tensioned to shape the sail properly, and we were ready to sail again.

We fell off of the wind and began another broad reach. I noted that while we dealt with *Summer Heat*'s sail plan, the fleet was being blown in all directions. Some boats had done just as we had and headed up to reef their sails, and others must have fallen off to accomplish the same task. All had been overpowered for a period of time. The tight little group was now spread out with only a few boats still in sight. That was to be expected in any wind condition and was not alarming. The wind was strong at about 30 knots and gusting once in a while to about 40 knots. The waves were building, and the crew was learning how to cope with the tremendous motion on board.

Shortly thereafter a disaster struck *Summer Heat*. Due to the chafing during the reefing exercise, the jib leech line began chafing along the edge of the sail. Quickly, the leech line tore half-way up the sail and flogged like a mad weedeater. Before we could react, the line had wrapped itself all the way around the jib and drawn itself tight, forming an hourglass out of the jib.

Now something really had to be done. I had Hannah take the helm as she was the third most experienced sailor on board and the second most experienced sailing *Summer Heat*. Dave Graf, an experienced sailor in his own right and the one who had been with me in the storm at the mouth of the Potomac River, went forward with me to deal with the errant leech line.

We were wearing inflatable PFDs with harnesses with a tether leading from the harness to the jackline. Before departing I had run jacklines (in this case, flat web line) from the stern to the bow on each side of the boat. The tether/jackline arrangement allowed us to move forward to the very bow of the boat without being impeded. With the heaving of *Summer Heat* it was challenging just to exit the cockpit and inch our way forward, always with at least one hand holding on to some part of the boat.

Upon arriving at the mess at the front end of the boat, we saw that the leech line was wrapped tightly around the jib and back onto itself many times. Damn, how could that have happened? Working together, Dave using one of his hands and me using one of mine, we eventually got the leech line unwrapped from the jib and the jib deployed itself with no help from us. One of us held on to the other and that person rolled up the leech line and tied it to itself. A better plan would have been to cut the line away entirely. Once the leech line was secured, Dave and I made our way back to the safety of the cockpit. I think we both collapsed for a couple of minutes while recovering from the exertion.

We had been on the water for several hours at this point, and the weather did not seem that it would lessen. It was time to initiate the watch system, even though all were excited to be on deck. While Hannah was first mate on *Summer Heat*, Dave Graf had the second most sailing experience of all of us and I made him the second watch commander. He and Jeff would stand second watch and Hannah and I would handle first watch. The watches rotated every four hours, but staggered so that one crew rotated every two hours, which allowed that oncoming crew member to rest (if possible) in the cockpit for his/her first two hours of watch standing. There were always two people standing watch in the cockpit.

Dave and Jeff went down below for their off-watch time. Hannah and I had been sailing the boat for a period of time when the wind rose to 40 knots and stayed there. It was past time to put in the second reefs of both the main and the jib. I intended to execute the process without calling up the off-watch crew, as Hannah and I had reefed the boat many times with no help, albeit not in 40 knots of wind. As I headed the boat up in preparation for the reefing exercise, the off-watch crew came up on deck to help. That turned out to be a really good idea as the boat was a wild place to be at that point. As the old saying goes, "one hand for the boat and one for you." The constant and violent motion was beginning to take its toll.

With the help of the off-watch crew, we were able to put the second reef in the main, and the jib was heavily furled with a patch of sail left deployed. Jeff and Dave returned to off-watch status down below, and Hannah and I were again sailing the boat.

We were still sailing on a broad reach. With the waves hitting *Summer Heat* on the aft quarter and the 40 knots of wind doing the same, the autopilot had long since been overpowered, and hand steering was the rigor of the day.

Another period of time passed, and the stricken leech line untied itself and again wrapped itself around the partially reefed jib. Hannah took the helm, and I clipped into the jackline, climbed out of the cockpit and inched my way forward for the second time that day. The motion was much worse this time around. When I got to the bow, I knelt down on deck and reached up with one hand to try to untie the leech line. Unknown to me, Hannah was having great difficulty steering the boat and keeping her under control. She wisely yelled down to Dave Graf for help on the helm, and he responded immediately.

Much to my chagrin, Dave elected to point the boat up into the wind. When that happened the bow plowed the trough of a wave, and I was immersed in green water, completely over my head. When the bow came up, I was happy to see that I was still on the boat. I had a death grip on the bow pulpit.

Summer Heat immediately plowed into the front of the next big wave, again completely submerging me. The water running down both my front and back was shockingly cold. I gasped for breath as I re-entered the world above water. I began yelling at the top of my voice to turn the boat around and made arm gestures to that effect. Before the boat got turned around, I went under for the third time. Believe me when I say that I was not a happy camper.

Once the boat was again on a broad reach, I somehow managed to untie the leech line and secure it to itself for the second time. I was precariously perched in a crouch, holding on to a stanchion with one hand while reaching up as far as I could with the other to tie the uncooperative leech line. All the while, the boat was heaving up and down in the heavy seas, causing me to be pitched forward, aft, and sideways. This time, I pulled it as tight as I could possibly get it. I then worked my way back to the cockpit and went down below to put on dry clothes under my very wet foul-weather gear.

I quickly returned to my watch and found all the crew still in the cockpit. As Jeff stood up to go back down below, a large wave struck the side of *Summer Heat*, causing Jeff to lose his balance and fall backward with nothing but air to grab. Jeff is a big man, and all of his weight fell directly on to the corner of the bench seat, squarely on his tailbone. Jeff slumped into the sole of the cockpit and his face turned beet red. He was in so much pain that all he could do was stare at me. He sat slumped for a couple of minutes, unable to utter a word. Then, without warning, he lurched forward and vomited into the sole of the cockpit. While I was very concerned for Jeff, I was also concerned that his vomiting would initiate a chain reaction in the rest of the crew. Conditions were bad enough that no one should hang his/her head over the side of the boat. They would just have to go in the cockpit, which was going to get nasty quickly. Hannah was prone to sea sickness and Jeff's episode was more than enough to turn her stomach upside down. I was almost afraid to look at Graf, but he was holding his own.

That incident altered our watch schedule for the next 24 hours. Jeff slowly got to his feet and after deciding that nothing was broken, headed for the bunk in the main saloon. The dinette table makes into to a bed, which we had already converted before leaving dock. Jeff crashed there, not to move for many hours. Hannah fled the cockpit immediately after Jeff, leaving the two watch captains to run the boat. Both Jeff and Hannah were in the vomiting stage of sea sickness.

The wind reportedly gusted to 60 knots during the evening and blew a steady 40 knots throughout the evening and into the early morning. The autopilot was useless so Dave and I took one-hour turns on the helm, which was about all either of us wanted to handle. Each wave tried to kick the stern of the boat around, which would have been disastrous if it had been allowed to happen. Had the boat been pushed sideways to the waves, a very real possibility of a broach existed. If *Summer Heat* turned sideways to the large waves, creating a broach, she may well have been knocked down, or worse. Wind gusts attempted to do the same thing to us. It was our job to keep *Summer Heat* in the correct attitude to the waves, which we did for a long time. *Summer Heat* did not have a full enclosure for the cockpit, but she did have a bimini, dodger, and a connecter piece between the two. With the wind coming aft of the beam, we were pretty exposed and getting cold.

That cold that I caught over the weekend and treated with cold medicine and two or three or four beers caught up with me right then. Dehydration. Sometime after dark, I think around 2000 (8 PM), my right foot cramped as I stood at the helm fighting the conditions. I stretched out my foot, pulling hard on the toes and the cramp subsided. Shortly, the left foot did the same. I got rid of that cramp in the same manner. Then the cramps moved to my hands, one at a time. I do not ever remember having cramps in my hands before or since that episode. I had to get these cramps under control as I could not abandon Dave Graf to helm the boat alone for the rest of the night by himself.

Jeff, who was still down for the count, somehow heard the discussion about remedying the cramps and yelled up the companionway that he had some Gatorade in the refrigerator. Really? I went to the refrigerator as fast as I could and found the Gatorade and quickly downed a bottle. I then ate a couple of bananas. Within a short time the cramps were gone and did not return. While I was in the galley, Jeff said that he was going to get up and help out in the cockpit. I checked on Hannah in the aft cabin and she was not ready to come up, nor was Jeff. That was wishful thinking on his part. As soon as his head came off the pillow, he collapsed right back down. Graf and I would have to manage on our own.

We took turns sitting in the companionway, leaning against the bulkhead, facing aft, watching the helmsman. The companionway area allowed one to get somewhat out of the wind and afforded some rest. Each hour on the helm seemed like an eternity while the time in the companionway flew by. Several times during the evening Jeff said that he was ready to come up, but he just couldn't make it. At that point, he did not have the experience to helm the boat in those conditions anyway.

Jim Favors scheduled a communications check every several hours on the marine single side band radio. He had contact with Commander Weather Service, the professional weather router for the rally, who repeatedly said that the wind should be far less than it was. By late night the weather reports were becoming something of a joke but not funny.

Sometime after midnight, probably around 0200, the wind began to abate somewhat. I had been praying for that since we first got in trouble that afternoon. At 0400 I went down below and told Hannah that she would have to get up and relieve someone as Dave and I were both exhausted to the bone. She bravely agreed, saying that she was ready, and up she went. Jeff rallied at the same time and came up for air.

Dave Graf wanted me to take a break as I was responsible for navigation as well as everything else. He said that he could stay up a bit longer, so I went to the aft cabin and slept for almost three hours. The wind continued to diminish, and Dave Graf was able to go off watch as well. The autopilot was again in control of the steering, and Hannah and Jeff were able to stand a full watch.

CHAPTER 35
DAY 2

BY 0700 THE WIND was down to 10 to 15 knots as I returned to the cockpit. The second day was a day of evaluating damage, trying to recover physically, and motor sailing. Eating was already an issue. Hannah had cooked several meals and froze them before we left home. All she had to do was heat them on the stove. We had food that we could have cooked and we had lettuce, tomatoes, ham, turkey, roast beef, mustard and mayonnaise for sandwiches. We also had milk and cereal. The problem was that Jeff and Hannah were still seasick and still vomiting once in a while. Graf was not hungry and I was famished, but I did not have the energy to deal with making food. I ate two PowerBars at a time throughout the day and they did well at sustaining me. Fortunately we had many PowerBars.

The first issue that had to be dealt with on that second day was the damaged jib. The wind was down, but the seas were still stirred up, and Dave Graf and I cautiously made our way forward to see what must be done. We were, of course, still clipped in to the jacklines, a rule we honored whenever we were above deck. As we approached the bow, we saw a pod of dolphins playing in our bow wave. I watched them for a few minutes then felt the urge to get to work on the damage. The dolphins stayed for at least a half-hour, and I would have watched them for the duration any other time.

We untied the leech line from the furled jib, cut off what had become excess line, and secured the remainder so that more tearing would not happen. The tear, at that point, was so high up the sail that we could barely reach the line to secure it. Surveying the jib, we saw that the heavy-duty nylon re-enforcement straps at the clew had chafed through on each side of the sail, leaving very little strength in the clew of the sail. The jib sheets, of course, attach to the clew and the re-enforcing straps are needed to help distribute the extreme force on that small corner of the sail. That chafing must have happened during the short time that the jib flogged during the reefing exercises of the previous day. I was truly amazed at how fast damage can occur in 40-plus knots of wind.

With the damage to the jib, we knew that we would be using that sail sparingly until it could be repaired in the Bahamas. We had stowed the jib sheets the previous night when the jib was in the hourglass configuration. We re-ran the sheets to have them ready for use when needed.

Based on the damage to the jib, I surveyed all running rigging and as much of the mainsail that I could get to. Both surprisingly and disappointingly, I discovered chafe on the first, or lower, reefing line. The line ran down the side of the mast for a short length and was held close to the mast by a small, curved, and smoothly polished piece of stainless steel. It was formed somewhat like the crook in one's finger, to hold the line in place, loosely. The high wind of the night before set up a vibration in the line, which, in turn, caused the chafing all the way through the sleeve of the line and into the core of the line. With the main reefed all evening, that number one reefing line was bar tight. I was surprised that it could move enough to chafe at all. After that, our only choice was to sail with all of the main flying or reefed down to the second reef point. Clearly on this second day, the entire main was deployed and the engine was engaged as the wind dropped to 10 knots and less.

More damage involved the $2,000 repeater screen that I had purchased at the Annapolis boat show just before departure. This "water resistant" device with a plastic cover over it ceased to function on this day, never to work again. The screen was mounted in the cockpit on the binnacle. Fortunately, I still had the computer down at the navigation station and would just have to run down there to check on our location.

Two boats dropped out of the rally and headed for Charleston, South Carolina. One had blown out both sails, and the other could not get his engine to start. Most of the boats had sustained some type of damage that first day. Thinking about the damaged jib and the chafe to the main's reefing line, coupled with the impending front that was forming below the Bahamas, I thought about going to Charleston too. Sixteen boats were continuing, and I again allowed "group think" to override my "little voice."

Jeff called from down below and announced that Jammer had urinated on the rug in the main saloon. Great. Hannah had purchased scented "pee pads" before we left, and I placed one in the head area of the boat and showed it to Jammer before we left. I took Jam into the head and again showed him the pad. This time, I urinated on it with him watching. He was a smart dog, and I hoped this would do the trick. Believe it or not, there were no more rug problems; Jammer started using the pad.

Sometime around mid-day I went down for my off-watch break. I told Dave Graf to sail if he could, but not so slowly as to drop behind the fleet. Fuel use was an issue as *Summer Heat* carried only thirty gallons in her tank. We had another thirty gallons in jerry cans on deck, held in reserve. When I interviewed Jim Favors before the trip, I asked him about the small size of *Summer Heat*'s internal tank. His response was "Hopefully, we will be sailing and it won't be an issue." He followed up saying that the thirty gallon tank would not be an issue.

I got about three hours of sleep, and when I came up on deck I discovered that we had been sailing at 3 to 4 knots and had dropped way back. I re-started the engine and began motor sailing again. While not an issue at that time, the angle of heel with the engine running would become very problematic later. The Yanmar engine was not to be run with a heel of more than seventeen degrees for any period of time. The reason for that limitation was that the engine oil would not be picked up from the bottom of the sump if the engine tilted more than seventeen degrees.

It was now 1600, and Hannah and Jeff were still "green" enough that they could not eat. Graf munched on a packet of nabs once in a while. I gave the PowerBars a good work out whenever I was hungry. No one wanted to dig into the refrigerator to make sandwiches.

The wind switched to the south and was building. The motion had never really stopped and now it was increasing again. Jim Favors' weather report from Commander Weather said that the wind would be from the south (on the nose), at 15 to 20 knots and then would switch to the southwest. From the southwest, we could sail and save fuel.

The wind increased to 25 to 30 knots out of the south, and the seas continued to build. The motion was incessant. The crew always had to brace themselves and always hold on to something, even when sitting in the cockpit. Everyone was tired and running low on human fuel. That evening I called the *Heart of Texas* on the radio to see how they were doing. Rankin responded and said that they had just finished a wonderful steak, baked potatoes, and salad with a glass of merlot. He said he was sitting back and enjoying a cigar as we spoke. My mouth dropped open. "How could they do that?" I could not believe that a forty-five-foot boat could make that much difference. They even had cake! Months later I learned that Rankin was kidding. His second mate, Jerry, was so seasick that he stayed in bed.

We pounded along, slamming hard when a wave would drop us without warning. Jim's weather reports from Commander Weather were not encouraging. Jim began talking about the now big front that had in fact formed below the Bahamas and was heading our way. He kept saying that we needed to "beat feet" south as quickly as possible in order to get in to Marsh Harbor before the front. The only good news was that the wind was to switch to the southwest and then the west, which would blow us to the Bahamas. At this point, rally participants had demoted Commander Weather to "Corporal Weather." We had little confidence in what they had to say.

The night was uneventful but quite uncomfortable. We always held on to something. Everything was a struggle. To go to the bathroom, one had to first unhook one's tether from the cockpit while holding on to a grab rail with the other hand, climb down the companionway stairs backward, find a grab rail down below, sit down and plant one's feet, take off the inflatable PFD, take off the foul-weather gear, scurry into the bathroom and finish removing enough clothes to do the job, try to do the job, and then reverse what one had just done. Believe me; we did not go to the bathroom unless it was absolutely necessary.

Summer Heat motor-sailed through the night with the main double reefed. Just reefing the sail was a major effort with the crew's fatigue and extreme motion of the boat. Motoring was now an issue. The wind screaming at 30 knots caused the angle of heel to be more than

17 degrees unless we slowed the engine. We were getting help from the main, plus the sail helped with the motion, so we wanted to keep the main flying. We could do only about 4 knots, as anything faster would cause excessive heeling, which was not acceptable with the engine running. The best situation was to motor-sail, not just sail (wind on the nose) and not just motor. On we went into the night. Our watch standing held up, and everyone got a few hours of sleep. Jammer was sequestered in the aft stateroom. As conditions worsened he moved to the bathroom where he could brace himself better.

Sleeping was challenging for all of us due to the pounding motion and the noise of the engine and wind. A person could not hold still on a bunk, as an arm, leg, head, or all would involuntarily lift off of the bed with each rise and fall of *Summer Heat*. Hannah and I both liked the aft stateroom, even with the noise of the engine. Jeff definitely liked the bunk in the main saloon. The v-berth was untenable. Dave Graf didn't seem to care and took whatever was available.

Jeff and Dave's personal gear migrated to the sole (floor) in the main saloon and into the sole forward at the v-berth. Anything and everything that had not been properly secured was now on the floor. In the main saloon, we literally walked on top of a foot of stuff. Walking in that area was already hazardous enough with all of the motion, and we did not need the obstacle course.

CHAPTER 36
DAY 3, "ARE YOU THINKING WHAT I AM THINKING?"

DAY THREE BEGAN with the wind still blowing form the south at twenty-five to thirty knots and, yes, the wind was on our nose. I went forward once again to check the standing rigging. I found chafe at the second reefing line on the mainsail. The chafe was caused by the same capturing device that caused the chafing on the first reefing line. Could this be a poor design? The chafing of the second reef line was a problem in that we were sailing double reefed and were relying on that reefing line to hold the second reef in place. If the line were to chafe all the way through, the main would immediately fully deploy itself in conditions that required the sail to be reefed down to the second reefing point.

I needed to devise a plan to set a permanent reef in the sail. We devoted one to two hours to creating a jury-rigged reef for the main. I located a small diameter line and lashed down the front reefing point to the front of the boom. When I tied the clew (aft end) reefing point to the boom and released tension from the original reefing line, a gap was created between the reefing point and the boom. This caused very poor sail shape and allowed too much sail to be deployed. What to do?

After thinking about it for a few minutes, I tied a second line to the aft reefing cringle, ran it through a turning point on the boom and then over to a jib winch, and cranked on the winch until the clew of the mainsail at the second reefing point had been pulled tight against the boom. Obviously, I could not leave the sail and boom with a line running to the winch, so I lashed another line around the reefed sail and boom, which served to hold the aft end of the sail tightly in place. I then removed the line from the winch and boom. The main was effectively reefed at the second reef point with nothing to chafe. This reef would not be shaken out unless we were sure that the weather had in fact moderated. This was not to be the case.

Another issue continued to plague us. This was day three, and no one had eaten a real meal. Dave Graf occasionally forced down a nab cracker, and I continued to eat PowerBars, generally two at a time, but Hannah and Jeff had eaten nothing. We were still pounding into large seas with the wind at 25 to 30 knots with thirty being more frequent.

Near noon I told Hannah that the crew really needed to eat some real food and that she and Jeff in particular needed to eat. Could she manage to heat up one of the meals that she had frozen before we left home? Hannah said that she was stable enough to do that, so down to the galley she went. This would be no easy task as the boat continued to pitch, bang, and roll.

After Hannah had been in the galley for a while I went down to check on her. I will never forget what I saw: one very brave and determined woman at the stove, stirring the contents of the pot with one hand and holding a partially full barf bag in the other hand while bracing herself with her legs and hips so that she did not fall. That is tough!

When I returned to the cockpit, Dave asked, "What's that smell?" I told him that Hannah was cooking lunch. I didn't tell him about the vomit or the fact that one pot of food was scorched, thus the odd smell. Yes, Hannah had to start a second pot of food, as the first was ruined.

She had cooked a very good chicken casserole, and everyone managed to get some of it down. I ate a large serving and went back for more. I told Hannah that I would perform the cleanup duties, and I am sure that she was relieved not to have to go right back down to the galley. The scorched Corning Ware pot had about an inch of heavily scorched food "glued" to the bottom. With the help of a butter knife I began digging the burnt offering out of the bottom of the pot. A full half-hour later I had the bottom scraped clean. There were several inches of loose scrapings in the pot, and that was not something that any of us would want to smell for the remainder of the trip. It needed to go.

I climbed up the companionway stairs with the pot in one hand while I balanced with the other. Entering the cockpit, I made my way to the side of the boat, kneeling on the seat. I was about to dump the scrapings overboard when Dave Graf said, "Here, let me do that." I thought, "I'm right here and about to dump it, but if he wants to do it, that's fine." I handed the pot to Dave and he asked, "You thinking what I'm thinking?" I replied, "Yeah."

I was dumbfounded as to what happened next. Dave quickly moved to the stern of *Summer Heat*, where I thought he was going to dump the ingredients, but, no, with a quick flick of his wrist, he intentionally threw the whole Corning Ware pot overboard! I watched the pot quickly sink into the deep blue sea and disappear from sight.

Stunned and very tired, I blurted out, "What the (bleep) are you doing?" Dave looked at me with this incredulous expression and said "I asked you if you were thinking what I was thinking."

"Dave, I just spent half an hour scraping the bottom of that pot, do you really think I wanted to throw the pot overboard?"

I guess that was a dumb question since he clearly did think I wanted to throw the pot away. It was a perfectly good pot and now we had one less pot on board.

Years later, Dave and I re-enacted that scene with a video camera and a broken Corning Ware pot.

Whether we wanted to or not, it was time to transfer fuel from the jerry cans into the boat's fuel tank. This would be quite a feat. The three guys clipped into the jackline, climbed out of the cockpit, and moved forward to retrieve two of the plastic fuel containers that were lashed forward of the mast. Two containers had to be untied and the remaining containers re-tied before continuing.

Jeff and Dave carried the two containers aft while I finished re-tying the other containers. Moving those cans was not easy with the pitching of the boat; again, it was one hand for you and one hand for the boat.

I had purchased a small hand pump before the trip. The pump screwed into the spout of the can and fit properly. The fuel filler cap was located outside the lifelines on the side of the boat, near the aft end. It really took all three of us to pump the fuel into the boat's tank. The jerry can had to be held at an angle while someone pumped the pump and someone else kept the hose in the filler hole. We had just enough hose to reach. The pump, of course, would not pump out all of the fuel, so the pump handle had to be unscrewed from the can and the can's extended spout attached. Then the can had to be lifted over top of the lifelines and turned upside down to insert the spout into the filler hole. Fun. All of this was done in 30 knots of wind on a very pitching boat.

This process was repeated with the second can of fuel. Those two empty cans were then taken back up to the front of the boat and tied in line with the other cans. While forward, we discovered that the vent cap had come completely off of one of the full jerry cans. The vent cap on another can was loose. We had to assume that the can with the missing cap had to be adulterated with sea water and was thus useless. We tightened the loose cap as much as possible and decided to hold that can in reserve and use it only if absolutely necessary. That was very bad news for *Summer Heat*, as it looked to us that the wind would continue to be on the nose, thus causing us to have to continue to run the engine.

I contacted trip leader Jim Favors on the single side band radio and informed him of my fuel situation. I said that if the wind did not change, I would need more fuel before reaching Marsh Harbor in the Abacos. It turned out that several other boats were having fuel issues too. Jim said that he had extra fuel and would try to rendezvous with us first thing in the morning. After dark we found ourselves in the company of another sailboat and determined that it was Jim and Margie Favors on S/V *Mahina Aka*. Good, this would make the rendezvous easy to accomplish in the morning.

The weather continued to dominate our plight, and the entire fleet was now referring to Commander Weather as "Private Weather." They just couldn't seem to get the prediction right. Whatever they said seemed not to come true, and generally the weather was worse than predicted.

CHAPTER 37
"DID YOU HEAR SOMETHING?"

SUMMER HEAT BOUNCED ALONG motor-sailing through the night. At 0200 I came on deck for my watch. Hannah was starting the second two hours of her watch, which meant it was her turn on the helm and I could stretch out and snooze a little more if possible. She was sitting to one side of the wheel and I lay down on the cockpit bench seat and placed my head on her lap. It was kind of romantic with just the two of us up there and for the first time in days, I relaxed a little. Within two minutes of my reclining, I heard aaaauuunnnnhhhaa, as the engine surged. I hoped it was just my imagination, but, no, within thirty seconds it happened again and that time Hannah heard it too.

"Dave, did you hear something?" she asked in her best Texas/Georgia accent. I sat up and said, "Yes, the engine surged twice."

Immediately after that, the engine shut down on its own accord. Hannah implored me to start the engine again. To myself I said that the engine was through. To appease her and hoping for the best, I re-started the engine, which lasted for about ten seconds.

"It's not gonna start again," I said dejectedly.

Jeff and Dave, down below trying to get some sleep, heard the engine shut down, restart, and die. They both popped their heads up through the companionway.

"What's up?" one of them asked.

"Clogged fuel filter, I hope," said I.

Hannah stayed at the helm and Jeff, Dave, and I went down below to tackle the engine issue. First we lifted the mattress in the aft cabin to locate and shut off the fuel lines. Having accomplished that rather simple task, we moved to the primary fuel filter, which was located at the rear of the engine compartment. The trick here was to remove the filter, spilling as little fuel as possible since whatever we spilled would not only make a mess, but also, we would have to smell it for hours if not days. That filter came off relatively easily and we bagged it, and then replaced the old filter with a new one.

The secondary filter looked a lot like an oil filter and was mounted on the side of the engine. That filter was supposed to be spun on hand tight, no more. I couldn't budge it. Jeff, who is quite strong, knelt down to unscrew the filter. He grunted and strained and his face turned red, to no avail. No problem, I knew where the fuel filter wrench was stored.

I waded through all the bags, clothes, magazines, and whatever else that had co-mingled on the sole to get to the storage locker located under the v-berth in the bow of the boat. There were four storage bins from which to choose. I went directly to the lower right bin, certain that I would lay my hand directly on the wrench. Nope, not there. "I guess it must be in the top right bin, but, I don't remember it being there," I thought. No matter, it wasn't there. Nor was it in either of the other two bins. "This is serious, I need that filter wrench!" Now desperate to find the wrench, I pulled every item out of all four bins just to make sure that I didn't somehow overlook the wrench. I created quite a mess in the floor at the v-berth, but still there was no wrench.

Jeff yelled up to me, "Did you find the wrench?"

"No, but I did find a big hose clamp that should fit around the filter."

Jeff put the hose clamp around the filter and tightened it as tight as he could get it with a large screwdriver. He then placed the screwdriver in the slot of the tightening screw of the clamp and tapped it with a hammer. The hose clamp began to move. Was the filter turning or was the hose clamp slipping? We weren't working in the best light. As suspected, the hose clamp was slipping. Why not, it was going along just like the rest of the trip so far. Jeff again tried to tighten the hose clamp and then tapped it with the hammer. It slipped again. Dave suggested driving a screwdriver through the filter and twisting the filter off in that manner. I nixed the idea as I was concerned that the filter would rip in half and we might not ever get the thing off.

Jeff returned to the filter with the screwdriver for the third time and I walked away, trying to think where that wrench could possibly be.

Suddenly Jeff excitedly exclaimed, "Dave, its turning!"

I wheeled around and said, "What's turning, the hose clamp?"

"No, the filter," a proud Jeff shared.

Surely enough we were able to spin the filter off. We installed a new filter, hand tight, and opened the fuel lines once again. All that remained to do was to just crack open the screw at the top of the fuel distributer and then pump the little thumb pump until fuel began to seep from the screw. Of course the thumb pump was in a very awkward place and required a lot of pumping to move fuel into and through two filters to the bleed port.

Once this was accomplished it was time to try to start the engine. We collectively held our breath as I turned on the key and pushed the starter button. The Yanmar diesel sprang to life. I put the shifter in the neutral position and revved the engine to 1500 rpm and let her settle in. I then placed her in gear, and we were once again underway. Of course, the off-watch's sleep cycle had been badly interrupted as the process had taken a couple of hours from start to finish.

CHAPTER 38
DAY 4, IT GETS WORSE

WHEN MORNING CAME it was evident that we had become separated from *Mahina Aka* during the night. We learned later that Jim and Margie had experienced problems on *Mahina Aka*. I called Jim on the marine single side band radio in reference to the fuel transfer that we had hoped would happen in the morning. Jim said that we would make a rendezvous sometime in the afternoon. He asked for my coordinates so that he could plot an intercepting course.

The wind was now up to 30 to 35 knots, still on the nose and not shifting to the southwest as "Private" (Commander) Weather had predicted previously. Jim reported in the group radio schedule that the weather was going to deteriorate dramatically during the upcoming night. Wasn't it bad enough already?

The system that had been south of the Bahamas would overtake us with heavy squall lines, storms, and high wind gusts. Once the front passed, the wind would diminish and move to the southwest and then the west, just what we needed to get to the Bahamas. The storm was predicted to blow past us during the night, and the following day would be a good one.

With the boat issues and the weather issues, Hannah and I discussed whether we should run for Florida. The problem was that we were right mid-way between our destination and Florida. We would get hammered by the weather no matter which way we chose. If we stayed with the rally, we would at least have radio communications with other boats. "Let's push on," we decided. I do not regret that decision at that time.

Five crew, four humans and one beast, had been using the one head in *Summer Heat* for the past three days and nights. Jammer had become very adept at using the pee pads. He might have had better aim than the human male crew. Since we had been in the Gulf Stream, the ambient temperature had warmed nicely. In fact, it was hot down below with the continuous running of the engine. No ports were open due to the sea state. Yes, the head was getting pretty odiferous.

Hannah decided it was time to clean the head and she dove in. The head area of small (37') boats is small in itself. There was not a lot of room to turn around in there, but even with all the motion caused by the wind and large waves, Hannah got down and scrubbed the entire bathroom. I really don't know how she stayed in there long enough to clean all the surfaces, but she did.

Sometime during the trip Hannah told me that while she and Jeff had been visibly ill, Dave Graf had been green for most of the time but was hiding it from me. Had Dave Graf not been on the trip, *Summer Heat* and I would have been in serious trouble right from the start. All of the crew, Jammer included, were troopers, but Dave Graf stood out. He had sailing skills that the others did not have, and he somehow managed his seasickness so that he could function.

Around noon on that fourth day, Jim Favors called for an updated position report. He said that it looked like we would rendezvous at 1400 (2 PM) and for us to keep a lookout for him. As 1400 neared, we saw a sail on the horizon. I was excited because I was very concerned about our fuel situation. Someone asked, "Is that *Mahina Aka* on the horizon?" I replied, "It must be, who would be heading right at us way out here?"

Jim called *Summer Heat* on the marine VHF radio and discussed the fuel transfer plans. He said that he had two plastic jerry cans, which he would tie together with thirty feet of dock line and attach a float (fender) to the middle of the line. As the two boats converged, *Mahina Aka* would be upwind of us and Jim would throw the cans overboard. We would have to approach the rig, cut the engine so as not to risk fouling the propeller with the dock line, and pick up the rig with a boat hook.

Dave Graf and Jeff went forward to the bow, again hooked in to the jackline. Dave's job was to catch the dock line with the boat hook, and Jeff would the haul up the load. My job was to drive *Summer Heat* to the two tied-together floating cans, slowing in time to not run over top of the gear, but keeping enough headway for steerage. Keep in mind that we were in 30 to 35 knots of wind and large waves. Hannah was to turn off the engine on my order.

Margie placed *Mahina Aka* about 25 yards directly upwind of us, and Jim threw the cans, line, and float overboard. He did a good job of keeping the cans stretched apart as he threw them. Now it was our turn. Keep in mind that Dave and Jeff were tethered to the jackline, which reduced their maneuverability some what. Dave got down low with the boat hook, having to negotiate the lifelines. Jeff was down, almost prone on the deck. I drove *Summer Heat* directly toward the cans and float.

On a close approach, I turned slightly to port (left) in order to put the cans to starboard, where the guys were positioned. I shifted into reverse, then neutral and yelled to Hannah to kill the engine. Graf reached down with the boat hook and caught the line on the first try. He pulled up on the slack of the line, and Jeff grabbed it. Jeff's strong right arm jerked sixty-three pounds of fuel out of the water and onto the deck. *Mahina Aka* turned away to get back on course, and she was the last Bahamas 500 Rally boat that we would see.

The two new cans of diesel fuel had to be secured, so I went forward to take care of that. When I returned to the cockpit Dave Graf suggested that we store the fuel in the forward stateroom to avoid getting water in the fuel since that was an issue in the past. I was opposed to the idea as I did not want diesel fumes inside the boat, nor did I want the possibility of diesel spilling all over the boat's interior. Dave campaigned hard to convince me otherwise. Finally I said, "There is one heck of a mess in front of the v-berth where the fuel would have to be stored. If you want to go down there and make a place for the cans to be stored safely and if you put the cans in trash bags, go for it."

Dave did not even have to think about it. He jumped up and went to work. We still had the one adulterated tank on deck as we had already transferred the one remaining good tank. We did not need more fuel in the boat's fuel tank right then, plus, it would have been extremely difficult to make the transfer under the tremendous movement of *Summer Heat*.

CHAPTER 39
NIGHTTIME OF DAY 4, YOU LYING MOON

THE LATEST WEATHER REPORT from "Private" Weather, relayed by Jim Favors, essentially said that we were going to get our butts kicked during the night, but that the front would pass and the following day would be a good sailing day.

By this time the crew was tired, very tired. For three out of four days, we had seen strong to heavy winds. The first day it blew a sustained 40 knots with gusts all the way to 60 knots. The wind dropped out during the morning of the second day but increased that night. By the third day we were back up to 25-30-35 knots. The fourth day was 30 to 35 knots.

I know that 25 to 30 knots does not sound so bad, and it isn't on many bodies of water. What must be considered, however, is the duration of the 25 to 30 knots and the amount of fetch, or the distance the wind blows unobstructed over open water, that wind crosses and pushes. The longer the wind blows at a set speed, the higher the waves become until they reach their theoretical maximum height for that amount of wind.

Even then, one wave can pile on top of another wave. Wave strength and height grow exponentially to the wind strength, so 30 to 35 knots is much stronger than 25 to 30. Forty knots is serious wind. From 25 to 30 knots and up, one always has to brace and hold on to something, even when sitting. The motion is never ending and very tiring. One's body is in a continuous state of tension and strain.

Since the first evening I had been praying, "Please, God, abate the wind." That prayer became my mantra. It would be used many times over during the fourth night and fifth day. Sometime in the afternoon, a feeling came over me that *Summer Heat* was not going to make it to the Bahamas. There was a sense of dread for a few moments, and then it went away.

As evening drew on, the wind increased markedly. The wind steadily climbed to 40 to 45 and to 50 knots during the evening and throughout the night. Once in a while the wind would drop down 10 or so knots, only to return with a vengeance.

Hannah and I stood the 2000 to 2400 watch. The wind was still on the nose and we motor-sailed. The helmsperson had to monitor the inclination, using a bulkhead mounted inclometer, to see that the boat did not heel more than the 17 degrees that the engine could tolerate. The helmsman repeatedly slowed the engine and then sped up in order to maintain 3 to 4 knots of speed. We could go no faster as the angle of heel would be too much. I allowed the boat to heel beyond the 17 degrees momentarily, as long as she returned quickly to 17 or less degrees.

"Please, God, abate the wind." Over and over I asked this prayer.

The night had been heavily overcast, and then the clouds began to break up and the moon peeked out from behind those threatening clouds. The moon was such a welcome sight. Maybe "Private" Weather had finally gotten it right and the front was passing over and the weather would improve. No, the moon was a liar, more clouds and heavy gusts attacked us, repeatedly. I was mad at the moon for lying to me. This has to end soon. But it did not.

At 2400 Dave and Jeff came on watch and I stayed with them for a while until they were oriented and comfortable with taking control of the boat. We all knew that this was a serious situation, not to be taken lightly. Everyone was concerned. Before going down for my break, I told Jeff and Dave to call me back up on deck if they needed me for any reason at all.

I went down below to the aft state room, removed my inflatable PFD, tether, shoes, and foul weather gear and laid down to try to rest. The motion was incredible. In a short while, I heard the on-watch crew calling for me. I reversed the process and put on all of the gear that I had recently taken off. I staggered through the boat and climbed clumsily up the companionway stairs.

As I clipped the tether to a strong point, Dave yelled (because that is what you had to do to be heard), "Sorry to call you up here, but you need to look at the radar to see the storm that is coming our way!" I climbed around to get aft of the binnacle in order to see the radar stand-alone screen. Yep, there, bigger than life, was Pac Man marching across the screen to get us. Heavy storms show up on radar as big black areas, which move across the screen in a threatening manner.

I remained in the cockpit with Jeff and Dave, waiting for Pac Man. The moon disappeared from view, and the heavy clouds moved in. Guess we are going to get it now, I thought.

Nothing happened, other than the 35 to 40 knot winds that we were already experiencing. After a while, the heavy clouds dissipated and the moon peeked out again, still a liar in my opinion.

As things seemed to be under control and the storm did not get us, I went back down to finish my break. Once again I went through the ritual of removing my gear. I lay down for a bit and then heard, "Tell Dave he needs to get back up here."

After donning all of the gear – boy was this is getting old – I climbed the companionway stairs and swung up into the cockpit. Dave Graf said that the radar indicated that another storm was coming, and that this new one looked worse than the first.

I took a look at the radar and agreed with the second mate; we might be in trouble this time, I thought. The moon again disappeared, and thick heavy storm clouds moved in. The wind increased over the 35 to 40 knots that we had been experiencing.

Jeff was seated, if you can call it that, on the port bench seat, Dave Graf was behind the wheel, and I was "seated" on the starboard bench seat. The wind had been primarily on the nose, but a very strong gust hit us from the starboard side, and *Summer Heat* heeled crazily to port, a near knockdown. That is when I heard "Oh no!" well up from somewhere inside of me and screech out into the cockpit. Fortunately, I don't think anyone heard my plea above the din of screaming wind and pounding waves.

Summer Heat righted herself, not quite experiencing a full knockdown. Jeff told me years later that when the boat went so far over, he reached back to brace himself from falling backward and his hand hit water and he could hear water very close by. I was shaken, but regained my composure as there really was no choice but to do so.

After that encounter, we decided to hove to and see how that would go. We hove to as best we could without having any jib deployed and were drifting at about 2 knots. The boat motion smoothed out quite a bit. After about 45 minutes, the immediate storm was still overhead and we thought that being hove to was causing us to stay under the storm and that we would never get out from under it if we stayed in this position. We pointed the boat back up into the wind and began motor sailing at 3 to 4 knots. At least we would eventually get out from under this immediate storm.

"Please, God, abate the wind."

I stayed in the cockpit with the guys and at 0400 they went down for a break and Hannah came up for her watch. I knew that the waves were large, but I could not see them. The moon was covered and the sky was totally black. I said to Hannah, "I will be glad when dawn comes so that I can see what is going on."

Be careful for what you wish.

CHAPTER 40
DAY 5; OH, MY BOAT

WHEN DAWN CAME, we saw everything all at once, and what we saw was frightening. My mouth dropped open, I am sure.

"Look at the waves!" I said incredulously. They were absolutely huge and all around us. The waves were mountainous. On one side of the boat a wave the height of a house on pilings, 20 feet, loomed, and on the other side there was a cavern the size of a football field. It looked like a very large salad bowl. These 20-foot monsters were not yet breaking, they were just huge, and then there was that big depression on the other side of the boat. Wow. It was otherworldly. How did we get here? Heck, last night was bad enough, but this was worse. I guess "Private" Weather was right on top of things.

Dave Graf and Jeff came up on deck for their watch at 0800. I stayed with them for a little while before going down below. This was a different ballgame, and we all knew it. The wind was blowing at 40 to 50 knots, still from the south. Would it ever switch around?

"God, please abate the wind."

After the second watch settled in, as best they could, I went off watch for a much-needed break.

Down below it was hot, as we were closing in on the Bahamas and the engine had been running for three straight days with no way to vent the heat. I went through the usual routine of removing the harness, inflatable PFD, shoes, and foul-weather gear, all of which were soaking wet. This time I kept going and stripped down to my underwear. I lay down, but it was impossible to sleep, no matter how tired I was. The motion and noise were incredible.

After some time went by, I felt the wind increase. Jeff opened the companionway hatch and yelled down for me to come up on deck. I put on all of my gear and foulies as quickly as possible, skipping the clothes, and struggled up the companionway stairs.

Another storm had been sighted on the radar. That was just what we needed. Dark clouds passed overhead, and the heavy wind buffeted the boat. Dave Graf, on the helm, did a fine job of controlling the boat.

After the squall passed we hove to. *Summer Heat* stayed in the hove-to position on her own for about 20 minutes and then she began sailing again. We decided to motor-sail since the boat was handling the waves and the wind. I went down below to resume my off-watch status. This time I kept my foul-weather gear on and lay down on the aft-cabin sole, too wet to be on the bed.

Jeff had taken the helm, with Dave Graf in the cockpit with him. Conditions were gradually worsening, and Jeff felt that he was in over his head. He later said that with the fantastic movement and the angle of heel, it took some planning and time to switch helmsmen.

After some amount of time, I again felt the wind increase and I could feel the strength of it radiate down the mast and shrouds. I got up from the sole and reached for my inflatable PFD with the intention of going top side. Immediately, I heard Dave Graf yell to Jeff, "Tell Dave to come up on deck again." I yelled up to them, "I'm coming."

Clambering up the companionway, I found the top sides to be wild. The waves were at least 20 feet high and the water was white, hissing with oxygenation. The wind speed had increased to 60 knots and *Summer Heat* began to shudder. The visual images were incredible, with white water everywhere, mixed with small patches of cobalt, the color of deep ocean water. We had to shout to hear each other. We were in an extremely serious situation, but *Summer Heat* was still holding her own against these radical conditions – or so I thought.

Within a minute or two, the top-most plastic sail slide broke, allowing the top of the mainsail to fall away from the mast slightly. A sail slide is a plastic or metal (in this case plastic) lug that connects the sail to the sail track and allows the sail to move up and down the mast when need be. A number of slides would be sewn along the length of the sail. The sail seemed to be stable, but this broken slide could not be a good thing.

I wondered, "Should we douse the main, and if so, how would we do it in this wind?" Most of the work could be done from the cockpit, although two of us would have to go onto the coach roof to tie the sail to the boom. That would be an extremely dangerous act under the prevailing conditions. *Summer Heat* was rising and falling with the 20-foot waves, and there was tremendous motion onboard. The flogging sail would be a serious danger to all on deck. Could we, in fact, control the sail long enough to secure it?

Within a couple of minutes the question became moot anyway. The second highest plastic sail slide broke, and the sail pulled farther away from the mast. Then, almost immediately, the remaining slides broke in descending order, like pulling down a zipper. I knew that we HAD to get the sail down, but how? The power in the main was incredible, even though it was double reefed. The thing had turned into a thrashing machine.

I told Dave Graf and Jeff that I was going to cut the mainsail loose from the boom, just above where it was reefed and lashed to the boom. I would have to climb up on the coach roof to accomplish this task. Dave emphatically said, "No Dave, you can't go up there! It's too dangerous and you won't be able to cut through the sail anyway!"

"I don't know how else to deal with it," I responded. It was clear to all three of us that we couldn't just lower the thing in normal fashion.

What did it take to have that exchange, 15 to 30 seconds? Suddenly the wild and loose main slammed into the port upper spreader and then slammed into it again. The entire standing rig shuddered. A spreader is a horizontal aluminum (in this case) arm that holds the shrouds off the mast and gives the mast stability and support.

The third time the sail slammed violently against the upper port spreader, the spreader broke at its connection to the mast. We easily saw the spreader moving forward and backward, rather than being stationary.

We were in big trouble. I yelled down to Hannah, who was in the main saloon, "Hannah, get on the single side band and call the fleet and let them know that we are in trouble with our mast!"

"OK, Dave!"

That took about ten seconds, and then the main began slamming into the port lower spreader as the sail slides broke away from the lower portion of the sail. Wham, wham, wham!!! Dave, Jeff, and I, all in the cockpit, saw the lower spreader break at its connection to the mast.

Then the strangest thing happened. At approximately one third of the way up the mast from the deck, the mast compressed into a "C" shape for a portion of the mast. It straightened and compressed into a "C" again. Then there was a loud bang, and the mast came down.

Yes, *Summer Heat*'s very tall and heavy mast came down, in an uncontrolled fall. Oh, my boat!

Fortunately, it fell to the port side of *Summer Heat*, with the top one third of the mast going overboard. The middle third was on deck on the port side of the boat. A stub was still standing in place. We were so very fortunate, no one got hurt.

We had been motor sailing and the engine immediately shut down, the propeller being fouled by some part of the mast or rigging that had gone overboard. We were in 20-foot seas with waves that were beginning to crest, and the engine was inoperative; thus, we could not control the boat, and because of this, we were sitting sideways to those mountainous waves.

I yelled down to Hannah, "Hannah, get on the single side band and issue a mayday to the fleet, then activate the EPIRB and bring it up on deck!" With a third of the mast being overboard and hanging down from the side of the boat, I was very concerned that the mast would slam into the side of *Summer Heat* and hole her. If that happened, we would go down fast. In those monstrous waves, it was crystal clear to me that we did not want to get into the life raft unless we absolutely had to, nor would anyone be going overboard to try to clear the fouled propeller. Jeff asked me if I wanted him to get the life raft out of its container, which was mounted on the foredeck. I said, "No, leave it where it is, we can get to it if we need it."

While Hannah was making contact with the fleet and, hopefully, the U.S. Coast Guard, the rest of the human crew jumped into action on deck. I asked someone to retrieve the bolt cutters from below deck, and I used them to cut away the remainder of the wires and standing rigging from the base of the mast. The top of the mast was being supported by the forestay and jib furling extrusion. If I wanted the mast to fall away completely from the side of the boat, I needed to cut these items loose.

I made my way to the bow and looked at the forestay, thinking, "This is going to be tough to cut." Then I noticed that the jib-furling extrusion, which is hollow and the forestay runs through it, was under extreme tension. The extrusion was bowed against the front pulpit and the weight of the mast was stressing it downward. "If I cut this thing loose, it's going to fly up and take someone's head off, probably mine."

Just then, Jeff asked me, "David, what happens if we cut the mast loose?"

"Damn," I replied. "The mast will sink into the ocean and most likely whatever is fouled around the prop will pull the shaft out of the boat and we will sink."

"Guess we are not going to cut the mast loose."

Fortunately, the mast was not slamming into the side of *Summer Heat.*

Hannah reached the fleet on *Summer Heat*'s ICOM 710 Marine Single Side Band Radio. A number of boats heard the mayday issued by Hannah and *Summer Heat*, to include Jim, the rally leader on *Mahina Aka.* Sue, the first mate on S/V *Kokopelli*, relayed the radio traffic to S/V *Dame Alicia* and her professional captain, Captain John, who had already made port in Marsh Harbour. When Captain John of *Dame Alicia* heard of our plight, he immediately, from land, contacted the U.S. Coast Guard. Within 8 minutes of Hannah's mayday, the U.S. Coast Guard contacted *Summer Heat* on the fleet frequency for the rally.

Coast Guard Air Station Miami advised that they were dispatching a Falcon jet to our location as helicopter rescue would be too far away. The helicopter's range was two hundred miles and we were apparently beyond that. The radio operator asked if we had an EPIRB on board and, if so, to activate it. Hannah responded that this had already been accomplished. The problem was that Hannah heard me tell her to activate the EPIRB, but she did not hear me say to bring it up on deck. It was still below deck where the signal was diminished. I had her bring the unit up on deck and almost immediately the Coast Guard picked up its signal.

Many months after this incident, Sandy Hollis, the first mate on S/V *Heart of Texas*, sent me a CD in which an amateur radio operator had recorded a good amount of the radio traffic between *Summer Heat*, the fleet, members of the fleet, the U.S. Coast Guard, and CSX *Horizon*. Radio traffic in script format has been transcribed from that

CD. Hannah, first mate, had only recreational or pleasure boat radio experience before this incident, but she did an excellent job in her handling of emergency radio traffic that day. As time wore on during the incident, I was sometimes on the radio. The radio traffic was over a period of about two hours. The transcription makes it seem far less. We pick up the radio traffic after the above contact:

> *Mahina Aka* (rally leader, Jim Favors): Where are you now?
> Other boat: Not too far from you. We're not too far from you. We've got nasty seas, big hairy clouds and winds blowing, gusting 35 to 40 some odd (these boats were much closer to the Bahamas than were we), and it's been going on for a while. I keep thinking the front's gonna pass, but, it hasn't and I heard you, and I am also wondering, do we have a scheduled talk or are we derailed, ah, because of the *Summer Heat* situation? Over.
> Pause
> *Mahina Aka*: Yeah Rick, I appreciate you that for us, ah, I know everybody is very, very eager to get in there and the sooner the better.
> *Shanty Irish*: Garbled -----
> *Mahina Aka*: Yeah, roger that. I appreciate it. Ah, we will be standing by, too. We lost our VHF radio last night. (The fatigue in Jim's voice was quite evident).
> *Summer Heat* (David Hope): Break for the Coast Guard, break for the Coast Guard!
> *Summer Heat*: Go ahead Coast Guard. (The urgency could be heard in my voice).
> Coast Guard: Yeah *Summer Heat*, Coast Guard 2113, be advised we are about six miles out. We're picking up your ELP, tracking inbound. We should be overhead in about a minute and a half.
> *Summer Heat* (David): Roger that. Do you need to see a flare, Coast Guard?
> Coast Guard: Ah, negative, negative. We'll track in on your EPIRB and we should have pretty good visibility, we're out here at, ah, ah we broke out about 1500' and we've got 10 miles from where you are now. Looks worse where we are going to, but, ah, we'll give you a holler when we get closer.
> *Summer Heat* (David): Ah, roger, I've also got my hand-held VHF with me. (The ship's radio was inoperable as the

antenna was at the top of the mast, which was now in the water. Fortunately, the single side-band antenna was a 23-foot whip antenna, mounted to the side rail of *Summer Heat* and not attached to the stricken mast at all.)

Coast Guard; OK, roger that. Yeah, we're getting a good strong signal from your EPIRB, so that should bring us right to you.

Summer Heat (David): Very good, thank you.

Pause

Kokopelli: *Summer Heat*, did you copy?

Summer Heat (Hannah): Yes, we are standing by for the Coast Guard to call us, so I just want to clear.

Kokopelli: That's fine, just letting you know. *Summer Heat*, they copied that. *Dame Alicia*, this is *Kokopelli*. Want to talk about fuel if we can at some point in time?

Summer Heat (Hannah): Please clear for the Coast Guard!

Kokopelli: I will clear.

While we certainly appreciated the radio assistance of our fellow rally members, it seemed to us that they sometimes forgot that *Summer Heat* had declared an emergency and needed the frequency to be clear for emergency radio traffic.

Summer Heat (Hannah): Yes mister Coast Guard, we see your plane.

Coast Guard: Eh, *Summer Heat*, roger that, OK, we're overhead and we'll stay with you, if you would go ahead and secure your EPIRB at this time, and, ah, let us know if there is anything we can do for you.

Summer Heat (Hannah): Repeat, clear the EPIRB you said?

Coast Guard: Yeah, that's affirmative. You can go ahead and turn off, turn off the EPIRB at this time.

Summer Heat (Hannah): Roger, will do.

Coast Guard: -------

Summer Heat (David): Go ahead Coast Guard.

Coast Guard: Yes sir, we were able to locate a fairly large vessel about eight miles away from you, ah, we've diverted them. They are en route to your position.

Sometime prior to the previous transmission, we had received a radio message that a cruise liner named the *Discovery* was en route to our location and would be on scene in two hours. My thought was that I could stand on my head for two hours if I had to. Two hours in an open ocean rescue is nothing, if the boat stays afloat that long. Would it?

> *Summer Heat* (David): Roger that. Thank you very much. ETA? (Estimated Time of Arrival).
> Coast Guard: Roger that, ah, we're estimating, ah, thirty to forty minutes, maybe as long as an hour. We are talking to them on channel one six if you would like to listen.
> *Summer Heat* (David): Ah, roger that, thank you.

With that, I turned on my hand-held marine VHF radio and monitored the traffic between the U.S. Coast Guard Falcon jet and the foreign registered commercial vessel in reference to providing assistance to *Summer Heat*. The captain or radio operator, probably the captain, spoke Middle –Eastern broken English. The Coast Guard told the ship of our plight and directed them to respond to our location.

The captain said, "Seas too big, wind too strong, cannot effect rescue." The Coast Guard responded, "If you want to go to Charleston Harbor, you WILL go to that stricken vessel and provide a wind shadow. You will steer a course of ---- and intercept *Summer Heat*."

"Ah you want me to steer ---- course?" said the foreign registered commercial vessel.

The Coast Guard responded, "That is correct!"

A few minutes later the Coast Guard again called the commercial vessel: "Captain, you are headed in the wrong direction! Steer ---- now!"

Again the captain responded back, "You want me to steer----. I will do so."

Once we felt comfortable that two ships were en route to our location, we began preparations for a rescue. Most of the water and Power Bars were removed from the ditch bag so that important personal items could be stowed in the ditch bag. Our passports were already in the bag as well as the ship's papers. Now wallets, checkbooks, jewelry, and my two hand guns, one of which was my retirement police service weapon, went in. I shot a video tape of the deck and the stricken mast so that the tape could go with us. After struggling to get the tape out of the recorder, I gave the tape to Hannah for safe keeping. She must have set it down to do something because the tape did not make it into the bag.

Two questions were weighing heavily on my mind. One, who would be able to make it in a transfer to one of those large ships, and two, what to do about Jammer? I was very concerned that we would have to climb a "Jacob's ladder" to board the "rescue" vessel. With the two vessels heaving up and down in 20 foot seas and with the exhaustion that we all felt, I did not know if everyone would have the strength, stamina, and coordination to jump to the net/ladder, hold on, and then climb up the thing. I was so worried that someone would sustain a crushed limb or worse, fall between the vessels to a certain death. I could never face Jeff's dad, my first cousin, if something were to happen to Jeff.

What about Jammer? This rescue would be a life or death circumstance for all of us. How could I get Jammer on board one of those ships? I knew that I was not going to leave him alive on *Summer Heat* to die a slow death of dehydration and starvation. I couldn't do that. I thought seriously about shooting him in the head. I knew how to do it as I had to terminate several severely wounded deer in my police career. Could I shoot my own much--loved dog, a member of my family? Rather than leave him alive on *Summer Heat*, probably so.

I sat below with him for a few minutes. He knew that something bad was happening. It was very hot in the aft cabin, but Jammer was shivering. I held him and said, "I'm getting you out of here somehow." I put his life jacket on him and then lashed a dock line through and around the vest, making a harness. I then attached a 30-foot dock line to the rope harness and to the life vest. If I had to, I intended to climb the Jacob's ladder with one end of the dock line tied to my belt. I would hopefully haul him up behind me. That plan probably would have killed us both.

After re-packing the ditch bag, we moved above deck to maintain a lookout for the ships and to get out of the heat in the main cabin. The tops of the huge waves began to crest and break on our heads in the cockpit. The entire waves were not breaking, just the tops. The wind was still up, and we had nothing to do but wait and worry about what would happen. While the five of us sat there, we said our goodbyes, in case the worst happened to any or all of us. Dave Graf told me later on, that when I said goodbye to Jammer, it was all he could do to keep his composure.

Family is extremely important to Jeff Akins. He looked at me and said, "My cousin, my brother, my friend-----."

Hannah told me later that she wanted to say, "Dave, if we get through this, let's get married." As my memory serves, she did actually say those words, instead of just thinking them.

Mahina Aka (to another boat): Yeah, we're ah, seeing 50 to 55 over here and we are south of you.

Summer Heat (David): Go ahead, Jim.

Mahina Aka: Hey, Dave, ah, is there a vessel en route, ah, I heard that's gonna come pick you guys up, over.

Summer Heat (David): It's a little complicated. They've got a cruise ship coming, that's about two hours away. But they've got some big vessel coming, ah, should be here shortly to make a lee for us. I don't think they are picking, picking us up, they're just making a, a lee of the wind for us.

Mahina Aka: Ah, roger that. Roger that. I know that will definitely help, ah, OK. We will definitely, ah, you know our thoughts are with you here and we'll definitely be monitoring what's going on, over.

Summer Heat (David): Roger, appreciate you helping us out and standing by.

Mahina Aka: Yeah, no problem. Ah, *Mahina Aka* standing by.

Coast Guard: Garbled-----

Mahina Aka: Yeah, go ahead Coast Guard, this is *Mahina Aka*.

Coast Guard: Yes sir, we're over here with *Summer Heat* at this time, ah, as far as the cruise ship, do you have any further information at this time?

Mahina Aka: Ah, that's a negative. Ah, we have some folks on a land base that, ah, that must have that information. We can give them a quick call, Coast Guard.

Coast Guard: Yeah, that'll be great. If you can do that and make sure they're still en route and also get the cruise ship's current latitude and longitude. The, ah, vessel coming at this time is not sure if they can get close enough to actually pick them up with this sea state.

Mahina Aka: Yeah, roger that. Let me, ah, *Dame Alicia Dame Alicia, Dame Alicia, Mahina Aka.*

Dame Alicia: *Dame Alicia*, go ahead.

Mahina Aka: Yeah John, ah, I got Coast Guard on, ah, 4015 (the fleet SSB radio frequency) regards to the cruise ship, was that a confirmed that they were en route? Over.

Dame Alicia: Ah, that is affirmative. Ah, they had actually, the cruise ship had actually contacted and spoke directly to *Summer Heat* as well.

Mahina Aka: The cruise ship is going to *Summer Heat*? Over.

Dame Alicia: Ah, it was about an hour ago they came up on our frequency and talked directly to *Summer Heat* and the name of the ship was *Discovery*.

Mahina Aka: What was the name of the ship?

Dame Alicia: *Discovery*. Like Discovery Channel.

The wind was so strong and the noise so loud that radio operators had great difficulty understanding each other. In conjunction with that, the radio signals were sometimes distorted and weak if the boat separation distances were not correct for that particular frequency.

Discovery: CSX *Discovery*, CSX *Discovery*.

Mahina Aka: CSX *Discovery*, this is sailing vessel *Mahina Aka*. We have Coast Guard on 4015, they would like to go ahead and confirm that you are en route to *Summer Heat* and also get your position. U.S. Coast Guard, we have *Discovery* on line. Over.

Coast Guard: Ah, Coast Guard monitored.

Discovery: Yes, this is CSX *Discovery*. We are first of all, not a cruise ship. We are container ship, single screw. Our position is: 27.32 North 77.02 West. Our speed is 21 knots, course 348.

Summer Heat (David): When you get on the scene, do you have a, a rescue plan that perhaps you could brief me on now so that we can be preparing?

Discovery: Ah, yes we do, ah, we're gonna come up to you and approach you and make a lee for you. Ah, this ship is equipped with a side port. Our plans are to have you board from the port side.

Summer Heat (David): Roger. I have one complication. I do have a dog on board. I'd like very much to bring him with us.

I wanted to present this issue in a manner that would not be construed as a demand, but rather an earnest request. These professional mariners were going out of their way to effect a rescue and I did not want to offend them in any way.

Discovery: We'll, we'll try to do all possible to bring the dog too, ah, ah, this shouldn't ah, yeah we're gonna have heaving lines, we're gonna have people ready, and, do you have anything to tie lines off to your boat?

Summer Heat (David): A, we've got boat cleats and, ah, things of, ah, that nature.

Discovery: -----yeah, ah, and, ah, the other thing is that, ah, the main thing is for the rest of you and possibly your dog, but, ah, you won't be you won't be bringing too much gear on board, over.

Summer Heat (David): Roger, understand. Can we bring our ditch bag with us?

Discovery: Yeah, yes.

Summer Heat (David): Roger that, thank you.

The captain of CSX *Discovery*, Captain John Hess, had set the boarding rules, and he or his chief mate was relaying that information to their radio operator, who, in turn relayed to us. The captain knew that time was of the essence with none to spare on anything but the rescue of people, nothing more, but perhaps a dog. The chief mate of CSX *Discovery*, Chief Mate Robin Espinoza, later told me that the *Discovery* would have only 5 minutes of stability in which to effect the rescue. Time really was of the essence.

Discovery: *Discovery* back to the Sea Heat (*Summer Heat*), ah, ah, there's no person that's incapacitated? Will they be able to climb a pilot ladder for a fairly short distance, say 15 feet?

Summer Heat (David): Yes, all people will be able to climb a pilot ladder.

This was a very bold statement, on my part, under the circumstances.

Discovery: OK, ah, how big is the dog?

Summer Heat (David): He's about 45 lbs.

Discovery: 45 lbs., OK.

Summer Heat (David): 4-5, just under 50.

Discovery: Four five, roger.

Coast Guard: Ah, *Discovery*, Coast Guard 2113.

Discovery: Ah, this is CSX *Discovery*, back to the Coast Guard.

Coast Guard: Yes sir, can I get your ETA to *Summer Heat*?
Discovery: Our ETA is one hour, approximately one hour. Did
     you receive that, our ETA is approximately one hour.
Coast Guard: CSX *Discovery*, Coast Guard 2113, roger,
     understand one hour.

Each and every transmission was not copied by the amateur radio operator, thus some of the traffic seems to not make sense, to be out of sequence, or to be distorted. One important piece that did not get recorded was when Jim Favors asked the Coast Guard Falcon jet to leave *Summer Heat*'s location to try to locate a PDQ catamaran, S/V *Tom Cat*, with whom communications had been lost in the previous day or two, not as a result of this immediate storm. *Tom Cat* did not have a single side band radio and had to rely on a marine VHF radio, which gave him an effective communication range of only approximately 25 nautical miles (nm). I could have choked Jim Favors for pulling the jet off of us, but I did understand his logic in utilizing that resource to find *Tom Cat*. *Tom Cat* did ultimately make it to Marsh Harbour, but it sustained structural vertical tears in both hulls where the crossbars fused with the hulls.

The last communication that we had with the U.S. Coast Guard was with the Falcon jet. Once it left the scene, contact with the Coast Guard was gone. Apparently the base station in Miami switched off of our frequency once the Falcon arrived on location.

As we waited, the following radio traffic was recorded:

Land base: The second group out, ah, plotted near where
     Summer Heat was, *Wild Goose* is kind of in that area, the
     group that is 80 to 90 miles out (we were 96 nm out).
     They're probably right in the thickest part of it now and
     they've just come through the thickest part say in the last
     hour and a half to two hours. To me, it looks like they can
     expect it to diminish, but it's going to diminish say over the
     next four to five hour period and they're probably look for
     their shift to come in about six hours. Ah, they haven't
     gotten into the ugliest part of this yet. They're still going to
     see from the 50 knots.
Kokopelli: Thank you. Again, *Kokopelli* will be standing by.

CHAPTER 41
"STAND DOWN, DO NOT APPROACH US AGAIN!"

AT THAT POINT, the foreign registered commercial vessel, name unknown, appeared on the horizon. I said to the crew, "They don't want to be here, I don't want them to try to rescue us!" I then thought about those words and reconsidered. A bird in the hand is worth two in the bush. Who knew what could happen during the next hour that we would be waiting for CSX *Discovery* to arrive.

The ship grew larger and larger. As it approached, seamen could be seen on deck, which appeared to be two or three stories above us. One crewman on the bow and one crewman near the stern had lines in their hands, the remaining crew all had cameras. To receive the lines, I stationed myself on the bow of *Summer Heat*. Dave Graf was midship, and Jeff was aft. Hannah controlled Jammer, the wonder dog.

The captain planned to steer his huge vessel along the side of our tiny one. The vessel bore down on us bow to bow. Amazingly, the captain maneuvered his behemoth right alongside of *Summer Heat* without running over top of us, but his ship would not stop.

As he approached us bow to bow, water suction tried to take *Summer Heat* under the side of the large ship. The side of *Summer Heat* was being drawn under the round sides of the ship! Violent collisions were happening between the commercial vessel and *Summer Heat*, and *Summer Heat* was losing the battle.

The cracking of Fiberglass could be heard all over my wonderful boat. *Summer Heat* ran along the entire 800-foot length of the ship, continuously being pounded by the hull of the monster. This damage was not a surprise to me as I had read about similar situations and had an idea of what to expect. The difference was that this was happening up close and very personally, and it was happening to MY boat! The two vessels were rising and falling at different rates in the 20-foot seas, which directly contributed to the devastation and the very real threats to our lives. Truly, we were in a life or death struggle.

One of the crewmen threw a heaving ball to me and was so accurate that he almost knocked me off the boat with his throw. Attached to the heaving ball was a thin, quarter-inch manila line. I pulled this line onboard *Summer Heat* as quickly as possible in the extreme conditions on the bow of the boat. I think I could have won any rodeo event that day.

I secured the line to a bow cleat and looked up to see that the bow of *Summer Heat* was rapidly approaching the stern of the large vessel. We were still being sucked under the side of the other vessel with each rise of that ship. I then saw something that I never want to see again: As the ship rose on the huge waves, her propeller would come half way out of the water, within yards of my location. It looked as though *Summer Heat* would surely be sucked under the transom of the huge ship.

I thought, "Great, the bow of *Summer Heat* is going to get sucked under the transom and I will get crushed to death and chewed up by the propeller, then the rest of my crew will certainly be killed as *Summer Heat* continues to run along the side of the ship, and under the stern."

As our bow drew perilously close to the business end of the commercial ship, a miracle happened with God's intervention. When *Summer Heat's* bow came alongside the curved transom and under sides of the ship, we rose to the top of a wave, allowing the full strength of the wind to hit our bow, effectively pushing us away from harm's door.

Wanting to get away from the immediate danger, I had to make my way to the port side of *Summer Heat* as the starboard side was blocked with inwardly smashed stanchions. I would have had to crawl over these obstacles without the benefit of the safety of the jackline, which had been fouled by the crushed stanchions. I unclipped from the starboard jackline and crawled to the port side and clipped in to that jackline. I then heard loud yells from Hannah and Jeff: "Dave, Dave, unclip, unclip!"

I looked around and at my tether and jackline combination and could see no reason to unclip. Again, with even more urgency and assertiveness, "Dave, Dave, unclip, unclip!"

The last thing that I wanted to do right then was to let go of my lifeline to *Summer Heat*. To unclip meant that if a rogue wave were to hit me or if I stumbled, I would go over the side without any attachment to the boat. I knew that even being attached, I would probably die before any possible rescue due to the violence of the ocean, but I definitely wanted to be clipped in.

Thinking that Jeff and Hannah must see something that I didn't see, I unclipped. I felt extremely vulnerable with the boat rising, falling, and bucking at such heights. I immediately dropped to the deck, prone, and began low crawling along the deck to the cockpit. When I reached the relative safety of the cockpit, I asked why they demanded that I unclip.

They said in unison: "Dave, we weren't talking to you, we were talking to Dave Graf!"

As the two vessels continued to move in opposite directions, the thin line that I had tied to the bow cleat was moving aft. The line had gotten under Dave Graf's tether and was working its way between Dave's arm and his torso. Hannah and Jeff thought that Dave's arm would be taken off when the line pulled tight, which it did. But luckily Dave's arm was intact.

At about that time, the quarter-inch manila line drew tight and parted with a loud bang with the line whipping through the air. Thinking back on it, I have often wondered if a larger dock line was attached to the small line and that I was supposed to haul enough line on board to get to the larger line. I saw no evidence of that during the event.

While I had been busy on the bow, a large diameter line had been thrown to the aft end of *Summer Heat*, and Jeff or Dave secured that line to the starboard aft cleat. When the storm wind pushed the bow of *Summer Heat* away from the ship, we began to swing away and the ship was continuing to move in the opposite direction of us. Shortly after the small bowline parted, I heard a very loud explosion on

Summer Heat's aft end. The large dock line had drawn tight and ripped the through-hull–bolted cleat right out of the side of my boat.

Shards of Fiberglass flew through the air, pelting Hannah, Dave Graf, and Jeff. I saw the cleat jettison away from *Summer Heat*. The force of the line being snatched tight jerked *Summer Heat* backward, causing the stern to slam into the side of the ship. The dinghy davits were bent at an awkward angle, with the dinghy dangling precariously. Before breaking, the bowline wiped out the dodger and bimini.

The two vessels were now moving apart from one another, the commercial ship under steam and *Summer Heat* adrift, heaving in the 20 footers. That was a very dark time for the crew of *Summer Heat*. Now the boat was definitely dying. We had to get help.

The big ship slowly began to circle around to make a second attempt. I was thinking that I should have listened to my "little voice," which had said to not accept a rescue attempt from that vessel. I radioed the captain and said, "Stand down, stand down, do not approach us again!" The captain replied, "You not want us make another try?" I said, "That is correct, please stand down, but stay on location if you can." The captain advised that he would remain on station.

I asked Hannah to call the Coast Guard to notify them of our current situation. The Coast Guard could not be raised as they apparently switched off when the Falcon jet left the scene. Hannah tried the single side band Coast Guard emergency hailing frequency to no avail. I said, "Call the *Discovery* and see if they are still coming. "I will Dave!" she cried.

Hannah called the Coast Guard on the marine single side band on both our "fleet" frequency and on the Coast Guard emergency hailing frequency and got no response. She then called CSX *Discovery* to ascertain if they were still en route to us.

> *Discovery*: (partial transmission), --- nine miles from the ship and we are waiting for him to pick you up.
> *Summer Heat* (Hannah): There's no way these people are going to pick us up! (In a very demonstrative but plaintive voice.)
> *Discovery*: We can't get in there right now with them there. What side, you located on their starboard side?
> *Summer Heat* (Hannah): They're actually behind us at this point in time.
> *Discovery*: OK, stand by.

Discovery called back and said, "*Summer Heat*, we are still en
route to your location and let me assure you that we will
execute a secure and safe rescue." (Not recorded).

Dame Alicia: *Summer Heat*, are they attempting to, to tow your
boat? Over.

Summer Heat (Hannah): No, they're not attempting to tow.
We're just trying to secure a line so they can get closer so
we can get a ladder.

Dame Alicia: Roger that. Ah, what they are doing is trying to
secure a line so they can get on the ladder. Over.

Dame Alicia was relaying information to other land-based people
as well as Jim Favors and the fleet. Everyone wanted to help, but at
that point, little could be done from offsite but offer advice. We were
in a fight for our lives, and remote advice was doing little more than
taking up valuable time. Again, their intentions were good and
honorable, and *Summer Heat*'s crew appreciated the offered help.

In another transmission, Hannah said that the ship was too fast in
its approach to *Summer Heat*.

Dame Alicia: Let me ask you a question when you say they are
"too fast" ah, does that mean they are traveling too fast
alongside you? Over.

Summer Heat (Hannah): Yes, because we have no power, we
can't control our speed.

Dame Alicia: (grasping for straws) Have you requested them to
slow down? Over.

Summer Heat (Hannah): Yes, I have.

Dame Alicia: OK, roger that.

Dame Alicia: They attempted to tie a line to your boat's toerail?
Over.

(I know that someone was feeding John these questions to ask,
but come on now, give us a break. We weren't just sitting out there
twiddling our thumbs).

Summer Heat (Hannah): We have no toerail.

(A better response would have been to say that we did secure
lines to *Summer Heat*, but in the heat of the moment and the
monumental stress that she was under, Hannah responded directly to
the question that was presented).

Dame Alicia: They have no toerail on that boat. Stand by, *Summer Heat*, they're trying to make a contact for the Coast Guard.

Summer Heat (Hannah): OK, they're going to make another pass, but we're trying to contact the Coast Guard. We are living in dread all the time.

Unknown: Understood, roger that. I'm just trying to get hold of *Summer Heat* to reassure them that we are working the problem.

We never did make contact with the Coast Guard again.

CHAPTER 42
THE RESCUE, CONTAINER SHIP CSX *DISCOVERY*

THE FOLLOWING TRANSMISSIONS are not recorded but come from my memory. It is likely that we switched radios at that point and conversed with *Discovery* via marine VHF. I was using a hand-held unit as the ship's radio was of no use, with the mast top-mounted antenna being submerged in the ocean.

> *Discovery*: *Summer Heat*, we are approaching your position now. Do you have flares on board?
>
> *Summer Heat* (David): Roger that, do you want me to shoot one off?
>
> *Discovery*: Roger that. We cannot see you with all of the white water.
>
> *Summer Heat* (David); Roger, I'll set one off now.

Dave Graf went below and retrieved the flare container and dug out a daytime parachute flare and handed it to me. I took the flare, tore off the top end, pointed it skyward, but away from the boat, and struck the firing mechanism with the palm of my hand. Whoosh, the flare ignited and took off in to the air. I was glad that I was wearing my sailing gloves, as the heat from the flare was significant.

Summer Heat (David): *Discovery*, I just shot off a flare, do you
    see it?
Discovery: *Summer Heat*, yes, we see it.
Summer Heat (David): *Discovery*, do you want me to set off
    another flare?
Discovery: No, we've got you now.
Summer Heat (David): Roger that.

As CSX *Discovery* made her approach, all 700 feet got larger and
larger, just like the other commercial ship. I had confidence that the
Discovery would be able to connect with us without further threat to
our lives. Nothing had changed weather-wise; the wind was still up
around 50 knots and the waves were huge. All we wanted to do was
get to a place of safety, off of our stricken home.

Discovery's approach was the same as the first ship, bow to bow. I
again positioned myself on the bow of *Summer Heat* with Dave mid-
ship, and Jeff at the stern. I saw the *Discovery* crew deploy a Jacob's
ladder over the side.

As stated earlier, I thought to myself, "Who is going to make it up
that ladder to safety? Will someone sustain a crushed limb or will
someone fall off and die?" "What if someone gets stuck on the ladder
and can't make it any farther up? Will the rest of the crew be stuck on
Summer Heat?"

The two vessels were rising and falling at very different and
dramatic rates. Regrettably, the attempt had the same results as that of
the first ship. *Discovery* was passing by too fast. Once again, the huge
ship's hull was crushing the starboard side of *Summer Heat*. We again
ran the entire 700 feet of the big ship, getting crushed all along. Being
on the bow, I again got a close-up look at the ship's propeller as it
lifted out of the water on the huge waves. Again it looked as though
we would be sucked under the stern of the ship and be crushed to
death. Once again, we were spit out, just before disaster could strike.

We were devastated. *Summer Heat* had sustained even more
damage, and the American flagged ship that we thought would deliver
us, damn near killed us, just as had the first ship. How are we going to
get out of this fix? *Summer Heat* was in serious trouble before the two
attempted rescues. Now, with structural damage, we had no idea how
long she could last.

Ironically, before the two rescue attempts *Summer Heat*'s hull
stood up to everything that the ocean threw at her. There had been no
leaks whatsoever. The boat had been dry. She was crippled to the

point of paralysis, but the hull had been seaworthy. Now, we HAD to get off. In my mind, we had to get off earlier, but now it was worse.

As *Discovery* pulled away, she radioed: "*Summer Heat*, we are going to circle around and try it again. It will take about 20 minutes to complete the maneuver."

> *Summer Heat* (David): CSX *Discovery*, this isn't working.
> *Discovery*: Yeah, roger that. This time we will get upwind of you, cut power, and drift down on you. Do you have running lights?
> *Summer Heat* (David): Roger that, we have running lights.
> *Discovery*: That's good, because if we don't make it on this attempt, you will have to turn them on.

Hearing those remarks, I looked around and for the first time, I realized that it would get dark soon. My watch revealed the ugly situation: November 17 at 1640. It was going to get dark a little after 1700. I said to no one in particular, "Damn, we can't do this in the dark, so far we can't even do it in the daytime!"

The atmosphere was grim aboard *Summer Heat*. We had to do it this time, somehow. No one knew what to expect from the huge CSX *Discovery* drifting down on us. Would she run over top of us? I'm not sure why, but it sounded like a good plan. It had to be better than what we had just experienced twice over.

The *Discovery* completed circling back into position and slowed her forward movement and began to drift toward *Summer Heat*. She loomed larger and larger, the hull getting longer and longer. That black hull looked massive.

> *Discovery*: *Summer Heat, Summer Heat, Discovery.*
> *Summer Heat* (David): Go ahead *Discovery*.
> *Discovery*: *Summer Heat*, this time, when we get close to you, we will open the pilot's hatch and you will enter through that hatch. You will only have a few minutes to get everyone onboard.
> *Summer Heat* (David): Roger that, thank you.

Shortly before the ship made physical contact, we saw smoke billow out of her smokestack when the captain put her in reverse for the final alignment. For the third time, I went forward to the bucking bow, with Dave Graf mid-ship, and Jeff at the stern.

Amid the maelstrom of loud noise, high wind, pitching ship and boat and the collisions of the two, heavy dock lines rained down upon us. These were substantial lines that would hold *Summer Heat* securely to CSX *Discovery*, and they were big enough that you did not want one of them to land on your head as it fell from the height of the deck of the *Discovery*.

A dock line landed only a foot or two from my position on the bow. I was able to quickly lash it to the starboard bow cleat, being sure to snug it before tying it off. I made my way back to the cockpit where Dave Graf held the end of another substantial line in his hand, looking for a place to tie it.

"Where can we tie this?" he asked.

Two of *Summer Heat*'s winches were located on the coach roof within a foot of one another. I said, "Here, let's lash the line between the winches!" Doing a figure eight with the line around the two winches, that line was made fast to the wild bucking *Summer Heat*.

The starboard aft cleat had earlier been pulled out of the side of *Summer Heat*, so the third line was lashed to the bent dinghy davits. *Summer Heat* was no longer moving fore or aft, as the lines held her in place. The rise and fall continued to be dramatic.

The time was quickly drawing near to abandon my beloved *Summer Heat*. I saw the pilot's hatch door open on *Discovery*. Inside the hull I could see people moving around. A female was directing the actions of others. It was quite apparent to me that she was in charge and effectively so. Immediately before the hatch opened I was called on the VHF hand-held radio by Chief Mate Robin Espinosa, who said that she was opening the hatch and for us to be ready to board.

The open hatch, which we later learned was only 4 feet by 5 feet, looked huge. Lights and people could be seen inside the ship. The hatch was a beacon of salvation. I was again forward of the cockpit. Dave Graf, near the stern, had Jammer in his arms. Dave yelled to me, "What do you want to do with Jammer?"

Time was of the essence and I yelled back, "You've got him, you deal with him – throw him!"

Dave Graf thought, "Throw him? What if I break his leg in the landing?" But with that, Dave pitched Jammer through the air like a sack of wheat toward the open pilot's hatch. Jammer flew through the air with his Springer Spaniel ears out like wings, just like ole Dumbo, the Disney elephant. I saw Jammer fly through the hatch, and I said out loud, "Thank God, my dog is safe!"

One down, four to go. Next was the ditch bag, which was given a mighty heave and landed inside the *Discovery*. Chief mate Espinosa yelled through the radio in an exasperated voice, "People, get the people!"

I was now standing just forward of the cockpit, on the side deck by the coach roof. It was Hannah's turn to go. The two vessels were rising and falling at alarmingly dangerous and different rates. In one instant, *Discovery*'s pilot hatch would be completely above our heads as we stood, waiting for the correct instant. Then, the boat and ship would be aligned for only a couple of seconds, and then we would be well above the pilot's hatch. Robin later told me that she could see our keel when we rose above the pilot's hatch.

This would be no easy feat to accomplish; one misjudged jump and someone would be dead. No question about it.

Hannah bravely stood on the narrow side deck of *Summer Heat*, waiting for the proper time to jump. A deckhand, Luke (unknown last name), was crouching in the open hatchway, waiting for Hannah to jump.

Hannah yelled to Luke, "Take my hand, take my hand!" Luke yelled back, "Jump, jump!" As the vessels aligned, Hannah sprang forward with an outstretched hand, which Luke, much to his credit, reached for and grabbed. Hannah's feet flew through the air and she disappeared into the hull of *Discovery*.

It was just about dark outside by now. Dave Graf turned to Jeff and yelled, "Jeff, you are next!" Jeff later revealed that when he heard those words, "Every ounce of bravado left me and I took off." I have never seen a big man move so quickly.

The vessels were still moving at life-threateningly different rates, and we were still in 20-foot seas. Somehow, Jeff's timing was not only quick but also perfect as he launched himself off the aft deck of *Summer Heat*.

One left for my responsibility. The initial stability of *Discovery* was gone, the alignment was more variable and the jump would have to be perfect. I was standing beside and a little behind Dave Graf. Dave prepared to jump. He crouched and leaned forward; a former paratrooper, he was ready. As Dave started to launch himself into space and the quite deadly area between *Summer Heat* and safety, Luke yelled at the top of his lungs, "No!!!"

I grabbed the back of Dave's PFD and pulled him back to an upright position. Dave got ready again, waiting for that split-second opportunity. He crouched and sprang again and again Luke yelled, "No!"

One of the dock lines was partially blocking the escape route. I pulled Dave back for the second time. Dave prepared again. This time, it was perfect – the third time's a charm – and Dave dove through the opening.

Then, it was my turn. An unexplainable calm came over me and I "knew" that I was going to get off the boat and that it would not be an issue. The two vessels had shifted fore and aft, causing me to have to leave my position just forward of the cockpit and scramble around to the other side of the boat and into the aft part of the cockpit. It seemed that it took only seconds for *Discovery* and *Summer Heat* to align as best as they were going to, and I dove as hard as I could toward that open hatch and safety.

It's funny the things that cross your mind in such times. I thought, "This is going to hurt." Meaning whatever I hit on the way into the ship will hurt, as the ship is all steel. In fact, I did feel my ankle hit the raised lower lip of the hatchway. I flew, prone, through the open hatch and landed on the engine-room deck, sliding on the wet and oily surface. While I was still sliding, two strong arms wrapped around my torso and picked me up off of the floor. A man's voice said, "We've got you, captain, welcome aboard."

I thought, "How does he know I'm the captain?"

Immediately, multiple hands were pounding me on the back and I was surrounded by the crew, who were all shouting and jumping up and down, and my crew, who were shouting as well. It was CSX *Discovery's* Super Bowl win and Olympic gold rolled into one. It was even more wonderful for the *Summer Heat* crew, and there was elation for all of us celebrating in that engine room. The hatch was closed, and I never saw *Summer Heat* again. Intellectually, I knew that she was gone but not emotionally.

CHAPTER 43
ONBOARD CSX *DISCOVERY*

THE CHIEF MATE said that she was taking us to another deck where the living quarters were located and we would have rooms there. She would get some clothes for us, we could get a shower, and in a half an hour we would be having supper with the captain and the ship's officers in the officers' mess. Wow!

Robin escorted us up two or three flights and dropped off Jeff at his own stateroom and did the same for Dave Graf. Hannah, Jammer, and I roomed together. The stateroom was Spartan with a metal desk, steel bunks, and a cold linoleum floor. I don't know when the last time was that Jammer had had a bowel movement, but he promptly relieved himself in the shower. Pretty smart dog, I think.

Jammer and Hannah took a shower and then I took one, the first for any of us since the night before the start of the trip. It was beyond description. Shortly, Robin knocked on the door and handed us clothing that had been donated by *Discovery* crew. When I got off of *Summer Heat* I was wearing foul-weather gear, underwear, and deck shoes, that's all. The rest of the *Summer Heat* crew was in a similar situation. Robin provided me with a set of white coveralls, and she gave Hannah a pair of her personal shorts and a shirt. Our few personal items were laundered at the ship's laundry facility and returned to us in short order.

Robin re-appeared at our stateroom and said that it was time to meet the captain for supper. She collected Jeff and Dave along the way and we headed down to the galley, where we went through the serving line. Rib-eye steaks were being served that evening, as well as a salad bar, vegetables, bread, and milk, iced tea, coffee, or water. The servings were as large as one wanted.

We entered the officers' mess, where we met Captain John Hess and members of his staff. It seemed that my crew's loss of appetite had finally disappeared. We were all famished. As I sat there at Captain Hess' table and ate in the polite company of his staff, I was struck with a feeling that I can only describe as being surreal, a very over-used descriptor but accurate to my situation. As I cut in to my rib-eye steak, I thought of the extreme contrast of being there, eating a nice meal in the company of wonderful people, when just 45 minutes previously we had been literally fighting for our lives.

During the meal and in conversations afterward, I learned a number of important things. Captain John Hess was recently assigned to CSX *Discovery*. Until two weeks prior to our rescue, the pilot's hatch could not be opened as it was blocked with some machinery. Chief Mate Espinosa said that the original rescue plan called for us to climb the Jacob's ladder as it was felt that it would be too dangerous to the *Discovery* to open her pilot's hatch under the extreme conditions that existed. The pilot's hatch was on the same level as the engine room and any in-flooding could be disastrous.

Also, the *Discovery* had only 5 minutes of initial stability to effect the rescue once the ship stopped her forward motion. This proved to be accurate.

One of the crew introduced himself to me as, "I am the one who held onto Luke's belt when he was leaning out of the pilot's hatch." That was the first time that I understood that CSX *Discovery*'s captain put his ship in peril and his crew put themselves in great jeopardy to rescue the *Summer Heat* crew. The only thing holding Luke inside the ship was his fellow crew member, who had him by the belt. Whew!

Finally, I learned that a sea rescue is not something that the ship's crew is required to practice, nor did they. The professionalism and bravery of the captain, chief mate, the crew, and the grace of God is what got us safely through the rescue. The rescue attempts turned out to be the most dangerous part of the ordeal, but no one lost his/her life, no one sustained a crushed limb, and the only physical damage to people was in the form of a few scrapes and bruises.

For four out of five days members of the *Summer Heat* crew prayed for wind abatement. While that did not happen, I am convinced that God reached down and tapped Chief Mate Espinosa and Captain Hess on the shoulder and said, "Open the pilot hatch for those people; I will keep your ship safe." Robin had specifically said to me that they had decided not to open the hatch due to the significant danger to their own ship. What changed their minds?

After supper, the captain gave us the run of the ship. Having spent the previous tumultuous five days on *Summer Heat*, one would think it would have been easy to walk the passageways of a 700-foot container ship. Not so. The waves were still up at 20 feet, and we had to learn to do the drunken-sailor walk on *Discovery*.

All four of us found our way to the bridge, where we observed Captain Hess and his staff at work. Later Jeff went to the day room, saying he wanted to spend some time with the crew who had rescued him. He told me that he kept falling asleep and that the crew told him to go to bed and get some much-needed rest.

Hannah and I went back to our stateroom and immediately climbed into bed. She took the bottom bunk and I took the top. Jammer was on a towel on the floor. There was little space between the top bunk and the ceiling, which called for one to be a contortionist to get in or out of bed. Somewhere around 3 or 4 AM, I woke up freezing. Man, I was cold.

I stretched one arm and immediately got a muscle spasm. When I extended the other arm another spasm shot through the muscles. Then both legs, one then the other, suffered a similar experience. I think the spasms were caused from dehydration and the intense strain that my entire body experienced throughout the rescue attempts.

My body was so stiff that I was having trouble finding the bottom bunk to step on as I bent over, exiting the top bunk. Hannah woke up and directed my foot to the bottom bunk and I cautiously lowered myself down.

Returning from the bathroom I said, "I'm freezing." Hannah replied, "Me too." While there was hardly room for one person in a bunk I said, "Move over, I'm coming to your bunk." The next thing Hannah knew she had another human and a dog in her bed. It turned out that the *Discovery* was experiencing problems with her heating and cooling system. No kidding.

The following morning we were awakened in time to respond down to the galley for a full breakfast. Basically whatever one wanted was there. I opted for a western omelet with all of the sides. Chief Mate Espinosa said that Captain Hess had offered the use of his personal satellite telephone so that we could make timely notifications, but to please make the calls short.

After breakfast I took advantage of Captain Hess's generous offer and placed two calls. The first was to my sister, Sylvia. My brother-in-law, Hunter Wright, answered the phone in Kingsport, Tennessee, and was very surprised to hear me on the other end. I said, "Hunter, this is David and I have something to tell you."

Immediately after that I choked up and fought hard not to cry in front of my brother-in-law. I got the emotions stopped and told Hunter briefly what had happened. I think he had a hard time digesting it.

The second call was to my boat insurance carrier. When the insurance company representative answered the phone I said, "I am calling from a satellite telephone in the Atlantic Ocean and I need to report a loss, please do not put me on hold." Immediately, I was put on hold. I waited for what seemed like two minutes and hung up. I called back and said in a louder voice, "Do not put me on hold." That operator managed to keep me on line and find an agent quickly.

The agent received a brief description of what happened and then asked, "Where is your boat now?" I replied, "As I said, the boat was abandoned and last seen at the coordinates that I just gave you."

""You mean to tell me that your boat is floating around in the Atlantic Ocean all by itself?" she asked.

"Yes, that is what I am telling you," I said.

"That makes me sick to my stomach," she said.

It didn't help my stomach either, and I did not think that she was trying to be supportive when she made that remark. She then asked, "Didn't the ship try to tow your boat?" I answered, "No, we were in 20-foot seas, the ship travels at 20-plus knots, and it was not their responsibility to tow my boat."

The last known coordinates were 28.00 degrees north and 77.10 degrees west, 96 nm NW of the Abacos. Only 96 nm to go, but it may as well have been two thousand. Having said that, we were very fortunate to be so close to the North Atlantic shipping lanes.

CSX *Discovery* was en route to Jacksonville, Florida, and was predicted to arrive in port by 10:30 AM. The seas had calmed overnight, and the ride into Jacksonville was pleasant. Some of our time was spent out on deck, watching the scenery of the St. Johns River.

As we closed on the Port of Jacksonville, we readied ourselves for departure, whatever that would be. I took off the white coveralls and donned my foul-weather gear, plus underwear, and returned the much-appreciated coveralls to Chief Mate Espinosa. Just before we departed, Captain Hess advised that members of the media were standing by for an interview and he asked me if I would speak to them. I said yes, that I would be glad to do so. Having dealt with the news media many times in my professional career, I did not want to talk with them now, but for Captain John Hess, I would gladly accommodate the request.

We walked in a row down the gangplank to the concrete dock. I had Jammer in my arms as we descended. Hannah, in her own flamboyant way, kneeled down and kissed the "ground" of the concrete dock.

Surely enough, several news microwave TV trucks were nearby. Dave Graf and I gave interviews, and in one clip I was identified as Captain John Hess. Sorry, Captain John.

The interviews took a good while to accomplish as there were several outlets to satisfy, to include CNN. I later learned that two of my sailing friends from Richmond, Virginia, were lying in bed that night, watching the news and reading, when Debbie exclaimed, "Look, there is Jammer on TV!" She actually recognized Jammer; this was not just any Springer Spaniel, this was Jammer. That is how my sailing group from Deltaville, Virginia, learned of the event, from Howard and Debbie watching CNN and seeing Jammer.

CHAPTER 44
GETTING HOME

UPON COMPLETING THE INTERVIEWS we were all wondering what would be next. "Is there a phone nearby?" "How will we get home?"

A full-size van had been sitting on the dock beside the interview area. I thought the gentleman was from one of the news outlets. He was not. He represented the Mariners' Mission of the Port of Jacksonville, Florida. The mission is staffed by volunteer RV (recreational vehicle) owners from throughout our great country who volunteer at the mission for a week at the time. He told us that he was standing by for us and that as soon as we were ready, he would drive us over to the mission, on port authority property, and that he and his partners would help us prepare for our journey home. The mission is religious based and is there to provide for the needs of the many mariners who enter the Port of Jacksonville.

We climbed into the van and rode the few minutes to the mission, a modest one-story building. The gentleman's wife and another couple were inside, waiting for our arrival. Once inside the mission and having met everyone, we were asked that we join hands with all present for a word of prayer. A prayer of thanks was offered on the behalf of the *Summer Heat* crew and for the crew of CSX *Discovery*.

The gentleman who had waited for us at the news conference turned out to be Bill Shutt, and his wife was Carol, who met us at the mission. They were from Edenton, North Carolina, a mere 50 nm up the Albemarle Sound from Colington Harbour, my home. We had sailed to Edenton numerous times.

They provided some snacks and something for Jammer to munch on, and then we were whisked off to the local Wal-Mart to buy some much-needed clothes for the trip home. Jammer stayed at the mission while we were at Wal-Mart. All four of us bought a few things to wear, and I still have my yellow sweatshirt and fleece pullover shirt to this day.

The van returned us to the mission, where we picked up Jammer and drove to the Jacksonville Airport, where Jeff and Dave left us to fly home. The airlines were kind enough to waive the change of date fees for Jeff and Dave. I had a 15½-year-old dog that needed no more stress in his life at that point, so Hannah and I elected to rent a car and drive home. I think that driving was good therapy and gave us a little time to decompress before getting home.

By the time we picked up the rental car it was late in the afternoon and I said, "Let's just get out of Florida and try to make it to Savannah before stopping for the night." We found a motel just off of I-95 at a Savannah exit and stopped. I didn't know if the motel was pet friendly or not, and I didn't care too much at that point. I smuggled Jammer into the room, and he didn't bother to bark at any sounds.

The following morning, Hannah and I walked to the adjacent restaurant for a full-course breakfast. While we were sitting there in the busy restaurant waiting for our food to arrive, it finally struck me as to what had happened to all of us and to my wonderful boat. The tears started flowing down my face uncontrollably. The faucet turned on and I could not get it to stop. People were walking by our booth and I was embarrassed, but it did not matter, the tears kept coming. I finally got stopped just before the food arrived and was able to eat some of my breakfast. I always enjoy breakfast and to not be able to eat it all was telling.

In the year 2002, a one-way car rental could not be dropped off on the Outer Banks. We would have to leave the car in Chesapeake, Virginia and find a way to get the remaining 70 miles home. I called my close friend, Dave Enochs, who at that point did not know what had happened. It took Dave some time to comprehend just exactly what I was telling him. At first, he thought I was kidding. When I assured him that I was not kidding and that the three of us needed a ride home from Chesapeake, he stuttered "Ah, ah, let me think what---." He was still not fully up to speed on this. Finally it all clicked and he said. "Sure, I'll come get you, just call me when you get within an hour and a half."

I thought that the drive from Savannah to Chesapeake would seem to take forever under the circumstances. Interestingly, it did not. The time went fairly quickly. Dave Enochs and I got to the car drop-off point at about the same time. Dave is not a demonstrative man and not one to embrace other men physically. When we saw each other and approached, he gave me a big hug and I think his eyes were moist; I know that mine were.

We put our few possessions – foul-weather gear, PFDs, and the ditch bag – in the van, and Hannah and Jammer climbed in the backseat. I looked in and said as complainingly as I could muster, "Damn, Dave, what is missing?"

Dave, completely baffled, said, "What?"

I said, "The beer, the beer, we always have beer in the van!"

Dave replied, "Man, you had me so confused and upset that I never even thought about it."

"Right, let's correct that mistake." A Styrofoam cooler, beer, and a bag of ice later, and we were ready to go home.

CHAPTER 45
THE AFTERMATH

THE FOLLOWING MORNING I woke up at home on the Outer Banks. I wasn't supposed to be there. After a quick breakfast, I got down to the work at hand, dealing with the insurance company. Since the loss occurred in international waters, my case was assigned to an international claims agent who was a nice person but knew nothing about marine-insurance claims. The beginning of our conversation went something like this:

Agent: I understand that you lost your boat in the Atlantic Ocean near the Bahamas, is that correct?

Me: Yes, that is correct.

Agent: Do you have someone looking for your boat?

Me: No, that is your job, which is why I called in the coordinates twice, as soon as possible.

Agent: We didn't know if those coordinates were correct so we didn't send anyone out to search for your boat.

Me: Of course they were correct, that is why I gave them to you.

Agent: We will see if we can find someone to go look for the boat.

After making yet another recorded statement as to what happened and after exchanging pertinent information, the call was concluded.

Within two or three days the agent called back and said, "I have good news and bad news, which do you want first?"

I replied, the good news.

She said, "Since the boat is lost, therefore a total loss, you will not be required to pay the deductible. The bad news is that your personal property loss is limited as is your electronics loss. Your electronics coverage is limited to $500. Since you were in a wind storm, you might be able to file for wind damage and recover your personal property loss through wind damage on your home policy."

I have wind damage coverage on my home since it is located on the Outer Banks, which is susceptible to high wind on a regular basis. It seemed that each time the agent called there would be a flip. On one call, the news would be good and I would be on a high, thinking that I would recoup a good deal of my loss. The very next call would bring bad news from the agent, bringing my emotions to a low. I never knew from week to week what to expect financially.

A follow up call from the agent revealed that I could collect only 10 percent of the value of my personal property loss since the loss did not happen in my residence. We were talking about thousands of dollars. My first mate, Hannah, would collect nothing since we were not married, nor would Dave Graf and Jeff, under my policy.

This was a very uncomfortable time. I had lost my boat and everything in it and now I didn't know what kind of reimbursement I would get, and it kept changing. At one point, the agent called and said that she did not know if the company would consider this event to be a wind storm or not. "Damn, if that was not a wind storm then what the heck was it?" I thought.

On the bright side, Hannah was working diligently on itemizing all of the items that had been on the boat. For example, we had 100 music CDs on board. At $15 a pop, that adds up. Electronics items such as radar, which cost $1,500, added up quickly, and I was to get only $500 for all of my boat electronics. Thus, one can see why I needed to claim all that I could under my personal property wind damage coverage. The 10 percent reimbursement really hurt.

Hannah contacted someone at West Marine's home office, who was instrumental in helping us reconstruct our West Marine purchases since buying *Summer Heat*. The items that I bought with a card were easy to document, but he traced even cash purchases for us.

Hannah typed 21 single-line pages of items for a total of approximately 300 personal items at a value of $26,203.60. Under my homeowner's policy, the maximum amount that I could have claimed for personal property was $72,100. Ten percent of that is $7,210, and that is ultimately what I received for my personal property.

Weeks went by with no resolution and weeks turned into months. All this time, I was making payments on a boat that I no longer possessed.

In the meantime, Rankin Tippins, captain of S/V *Heart of Texas*, called from the Bahamas to express his and Sandy's condolences for the loss of *Summer Heat*. Rankin, Sandy, and their friend Jerry, made it to the Bahamas, but sustained damage to *Heart of Texas*. For one thing, the rub rail was torn off one side of the boat. It turned out to be quite a job to replace the rub rail. Rankin graciously extended an invitation to Hannah and me to fly to the Bahamas after the Christmas holidays and visit on board *Heart of Texas* for a week or so. I thanked Rankin for the call and for the invitation and said that we would love to visit with them but would have to see how the insurance claim was progressing.

When we left home for the Bahamas 500 Rally, I left several sailing magazines on the coffee table. Upon our unexpected return home, I would not even look at those magazines, much less pick one up and thumb through it.

Three weeks passed. I was dealing with the insurance, Rankin had called, and some form of normalcy had returned. One morning I was sitting on the couch with the coffee table directly in front of me. I glanced down at the sailing periodicals, looked away, and then glanced down again. I tentatively leaned forward and picked up one of the magazines and looked at the front cover. Nothing bad happened. The thing did not bite me, nor did lightning strike.

I opened the magazine to the front page and read it. I turned to the second page and read it. I then read the entire magazine, page by page, and when I finished, I read the other two magazines from cover to cover. Craving more, I jumped in my truck and drove down to a local magazine shop and bought what sailing magazines they had.

After Christmas, I contacted Rankin and said that we would like very much to come for a visit. He said that a number of the Bahamas 500 Rally participants had flown home for Christmas, but that they would be coming back directly after New Year's Eve and that would be a good time to visit as we would get to see some of the people from the rally. We agreed. I told Hannah that since we were flying into and out of Fort Lauderdale, perhaps we could look at some sailboats while we were there. She agreed.

When we arrived in the Abacos, I found the islands to be every bit as wonderful as I had thought. We had a fantastic time sailing around the local islands and seeing what we were missing by not being there for the winter. On our second evening in Marsh Harbour, Abaco, a group of us from the rally walked "downtown" to the waterfront to a bar/restaurant by the name of Snappas, where we were to meet more of our fellow rally participants.

Two of the folks we met were Ian and Sue of S/V *Kokopelli*, who had been a radio relay for us during the disaster. It was very good to see them. The group grabbed a long table, ordered beer and food and listened to the local band play "rake and scrape." This can be any type of music set to the rhythm of a knife drawn quickly back and forth over the cutting teeth of a hand saw, and maracas are employed a well. Shortly, the couple from the catamaran *Tom Cat* joined the group. *Tom Cat* was the boat that had not been heard from in two or three days during the rally and which suffered the structural vertical tearing of the hulls at the cross member.

Several folks wanted to hear our story, what happened to *Summer Heat*. I told the rather lengthy, sad tale, and Hannah added bits and pieces. When I finished, I looked at my audience and saw that our friends from S/V *Tom Cat* had tears streaming down their cheeks.

To this day, when I talk about the event or when reading what I have just written, I often experience raw emotions. Anytime that Jeff and I or Dave Graf and I engage in the event, some parts get to me. It generally has to do with an act of bravery of one of my crew or the thought of leaving Jammer behind.

CHAPTER 46
REPLACING *SUMMER HEAT*

I HAD CALLED A BOAT BROKER in Fort Lauderdale and set up an appointment during our return to Florida before we left home for the visit to the Abacos. The broker showed us a number of boats in Fort Lauderdale and in Miami. We were looking at production boats in the 40 to 45 foot range.

It was clear to me that my 37-foot boat had been a wonderful sailing boat, but it was a little too cramped for the way that I wanted to live on a boat. After looking at several boats, I learned that a 42-footer was about right for my needs, and I could afford no more anyway, if I could afford that.

The broker showed us two Hunter 42-foot center cockpit sailboats, both in the same marina, a few docks away from each other. They were both 1996 model boats. The first was a dock queen, or floating condo, and the owner's wife glared at us if we even thought about touching anything. The boat appeared to be pristine. I worried that the engine had sat idle for years.

The second Hunter 420 was tricked out for racing and had participated in numerous races, to include races to the Bahamas and Bermuda. When we climbed aboard, I said to Hannah, "Now this is a sailboat!" and compared it favorably to the floating condo. Upon inspection, it was apparent that the boat had been sailed hard. I wondered how tired she was.

I truthfully told the broker that I had to wait until the insurance claim had been resolved before I could buy another boat and that I needed to see if I could get coverage after having a total loss on my record. Additionally, I wanted to give Carolyn Norton Schmalenberger, owner of Norton's Yacht Sales, an opportunity to show us some boats, since I had bought my first two boats through her. We returned home to the Outer Banks boatless but knowing more about what we wanted.

The winter of 2002–03 was awful in my opinion. I was supposed to be wintering in the Abacos on *Summer Heat*; instead I was struggling through the insurance-claim process for the loss of *Summer Heat* and struggling through winter itself.

I had received a call from the international claims agent, who herself was struggling with my claim. She said that there was an ongoing discussion that focused on whether or not my claim was wind related. If not wind related, I would lose the reimbursement on the personal property claim. I said to her, "How could it not be wind related, we were in winds up to 60 knots?" Once again I was on that roller coaster of emotions.

A bright light appeared on my horizon approximately two and a half months into the claims process. Keep in mind that I was continuing to make boat-loan payments to the bank on a lost boat. I received a call from an insurance agent in south Florida who said that he was a maritime insurance specialist and that my case had been re-assigned to him. He assured me that my case certainly was wind related and that I would be awarded that claim and the he would work diligently and quickly to finish the entire process in a timely fashion. He just had to get up to speed and things would move along. He was right; within two to three weeks and several phone calls, my claim was finalized.

When it was all said and done, I lost approximately $25,000 in the process. I bought the boat for $125,000 on November 30, 1999, and insured it for that amount. By the fall of 2002, the insurance company (not a maritime company) devalued my boat to $118,000 and I paid for coverage of that amount. This was not an "agreed upon value" policy, which I have now. That financial difference, coupled with the lack of full coverage on the personal property and electronics, cost me $25,000. I never would have thought that I could have recovered from a $25,000 loss, but I did. On March 3, 2003, the loan was paid off on my lost boat, S/V *Summer Heat*. It was a bittersweet day.

Near the end of February2003 I called Carolyn Norton Schmalenberger and said that I would like to look at some boats. She already knew of the tragedy. Carolyn said, "David, I'm going to do whatever it takes to get you back into a boat."

We drove up to Deltaville, a three-and-a-half-hour drive, to meet with Carolyn. She showed us every boat that she thought that I would possibly be interested in, to include a catamaran. Finally, she showed us a 2001 Hunter 420 center cockpit sloop-rigged sailboat.

This boat was the younger sibling of the two 1996 Hunter 420s that we saw in Miami. This boat was two seasons old and in pristine condition, just the way I like it. The only way that one could tell that the boat had been used was that a rug was in the aft cabin and there were remnants of a Budweiser box stuck to the bottom of the refrigerator. The boat's engine had a miserly 50 hours on it, and the generator had a mere 2.5 hours. The boat was perfect. It was almost new, and five years younger than the Miami boats. I did not have to go to Miami to get the thing, and I could buy it from a trusted businesswoman, Carolyn. The only problem was that it cost too much.

I told Carolyn that I loved the boat but I just could not afford it. I was not trying to take her down further in price; the boat was out of my comfort level. Carolyn negotiated a lower price and pulled in a favor with a lending institution with which she does a great deal of boat financing. She obtained this previously owned boat for the interest rate on a new boat "boat show" rate. I had to think about it.

The following day Hannah and I drove to Georgia to visit her parents. For the duration of the drive I thought of nothing but that boat and whether or not I could afford the payments, which would be substantially higher than what I had been paying on *Summer Heat*. That evening Hannah and I went out for supper after visiting with her parents and siblings. As I sat in the restaurant, I said, "I'm going to do it, I'm going to buy the boat. I may be crazy, but I'm going to do it." Then, "I'll call Carolyn first thing in the morning."

Choosing a name for the new boat was problematic. I refused to name it "*Summer Heat*" out of respect for my lost boat that had served the crew so well until a cheap piece of plastic did her in. Nor did I like "*Summer Heat* II." I have never liked the suffixes on boats. I could not tolerate the trite (to me) names on so many boats and felt that a name should be respectful.

I thought about incorporating my last name into the boat name. One night I woke up in the middle of the night and said, "Bright Hope, that's it!" But the light of day caused me to re-think the name. Bright Hope, hum, sounds kind of weak, like "I hope I don't lose another boat." That name was wiped from the slate.

A short time later we were sitting around, throwing out name possibilities. I thought of variations of *Summer Heat* and suddenly "*Southern Heat*" popped out of my mouth. I repeated it, "*Southern Heat*, I think I like it." There are a lot of meanings there. "Southern," we are from the South and love the South. "Heat," obviously homage to the lost boat and secondly, the South is hot in the summer and I love the heat. Third, it's a "hot" boat, and fourth, being a retired police officer, I was the "heat." *Southern Heat* it is.

Now I had another boat to outfit for cruising. The boat had a very nice, at the time, 10.2-inch color chart plotter/radar unit combination in conjunction with an autopilot. It also had refrigeration, a freezer, and a 5.5 kw generator. It needed everything else to be cruise ready. This center cockpit boat had a nice bimini top but needed all of the vinyl sides to make a full enclosure, something that would be very important when moving the boat in cold weather. Thus, the full enclosure was the first order of business. Additionally, the boat would need many more items. These were some of the items that were installed on *Southern Heat* as she sat in Deltaville for the summer:

Dinghy davits
10-foot hard-bottom dinghy (rib)
Chaps for the dinghy
15 HP outboard for the dinghy
Lifting davit for the outboard
Solar panels
Solar panel controller
Marine single side band radio and antenna tuner
Single side band antenna
Pactor modem for interface with the single side band
    and the computer
Computer
Navigation software for the computer
Weather fax software
Solas Grade flares
Storm jib sail and inner forestay

Life raft and storage box
Man overboard equipment
Type one PFDs
Inflatable PFDs
Jacklines
Storm parachute anchor
CD stacker player

CHAPTER 47: ARTHUR B. HANSON RESCUE MEDAL AND THE LOSS OF CREW

NO GOOD DEED must go unrewarded, and so it was with CSX *Discovery*. I had been looking for a lifesaving award that could be presented to CSX *Discovery* crew. After several attempts to find such an award failed, I stopped looking for a few months and then got back on the project. I found that U.S. Sailing had such an award, and after several e-mails I was connected with the correct person at U.S. Sailing to facilitate the nomination process, which turned out to be lengthy and involved. I wrote the nomination, which included the details of the dismasting and the rescue. Several weeks passed before I received word that the *Discovery* had been granted the Arthur B. Hanson Rescue Medal

The *Discovery* was no longer CSX *Discovery* but now the *Horizon Discovery*. Upper management was contacted and a date established for the award presentation at the Jacksonville Port Authority. By the time that the date was set, we were close to the one-year anniversary of the event. The four human crew members of *Summer Heat* were all in attendance. Fortunately, Captain John Hess continued to captain the *Discovery* and was present to receive the medal for the ship and crew. Chief Mate Espinosa had transferred to the U.S. West Coast for a well-deserved promotion.

The presentation was well attended and was a media event. We again toured the *Discovery*, this time at our leisure and without the 20-foot seas. After departing the *Discovery*, we walked her 700-foot length. Jeff and Dave stopped a little aft of midship and called to me. "Look here!"

They were standing in front of the pilot's hatch, which had looked so huge to us during the rescue. It really was only four feet by five feet and looked pretty small to all four of us. We were in awe that the five of us had made it safely into the hull of the *Discovery*. I was very happy that U.S. Sailing saw fit to honor the captain, crew, and the *Discovery* herself with the Arthur B. Hanson Rescue Medal.

Concurrently, I was making plans to take *Southern Heat* to the Bahamas for the winter of 2003–04.

In the meantime, Jammer the wonder dog suffered a stroke in the early part of summer 2003. There were no obvious signs until I noticed that he was not eating and could not lap water. We went to the vet and Jammer stayed for several days to be re-hydrated through an IV. I picked him up on Friday afternoon, and there was much discussion with the vet about euthanasia on the following Monday. I said that I wanted to take him home for the weekend. The IV did hydrate him and he looked much better. He still could not lap water. The vet, a wonderful human being, gave me a needleless syringe to take home with me to gently squirt water into Jammer's mouth. All weekend I gave Jammer water through the syringe. By Monday, Jammer was looking even better and it was obvious to me that he still had life in him and was not ready to die.

Hannah and I fed him hand–to-mouth for days until he began to re-learn how to eat out of his bowl. Drinking was still an issue, but I did not mind giving him his water by syringe. What a dog. Jammer continued to live as best he could for three more months. He would "play" by mouthing on my hand and chewing a toy or two. He liked being a lap dog for that time.

Finally, one nice sunny September day, it was time. Jammer and I sat in the back yard for hours that day, him just resting on the grass with me by his side. That afternoon when Hannah came home from work, we drove Jammer to the vet's office. Jam rode quietly on Hannah's lap. Dr. Burkhart met us at the car and said that there was a nice grassy area behind the building that was both quiet and private. When Jammer quit breathing, a sound came out of me from deep within, a sound that I had never heard before and did not know that I could make. Then the dam broke loose and I cried and could not stop. While I had driven us to the vet's office, Hannah drove us home. Jammer had lived almost 17 glorious and wonderful years.

One of the crew was gone. Within a year, a second would leave my life.

We brought *Southern Heat* to Colington in preparation for the upcoming trip to the Bahamas. Final outfitting was being completed, and a few sailing days were enjoyed. With about three weeks to go before the departure date, a business deal of Hannah's, which would have allowed her to go to the Bahamas for the winter, collapsed. I was a very unhappy camper. It looked like another winter would be spent sitting in the Outer Banks.

Rankin and Sandy of the *Heart of Texas* stopped by on their boat just before Thanksgiving weekend. I found a slip for *Heart of Texas* at my next-door neighbor's residence. Sandy went to her mother's for Thanksgiving, and Rankin went to his mother's. They would return on the following Tuesday. They invited me to sail with them down the coast and the Intracoastal Water way to Florida and then over to the Bahamas. I had nothing else to do and accepted the invitation. Hannah had to work and said she had no objections to me going on the adventure, which turned out to be a sticking point later on.

At first light on the Wednesday after Thanksgiving, *Heart of Texas* slipped her lines and started down the canal to the Albemarle Sound. Hannah waved goodbye and ran across the back yard with tears in her eyes. I should have figured something was amiss, but I did not.

It was quite cold outside, but the full enclosure warmed us nicely by 10 AM daily, if it was sunny. The nights were cold. We motored to Beaufort, North Carolina, where we waited out some bad weather.

Rankin intended to sail on the outside, in the Atlantic Ocean, from Beaufort to Charleston, South Carolina. Three cold fronts were predicted to blow through in the next 36 hours. The wind built throughout the afternoon and night. Sandy and I stood the late night/early morning watch, and we both watched the wind increase from 15 to 20 to 20 to 25, and finally 25 to 30 knots. We both said that we could not believe that we were back out in bad conditions, and of course the wind was on our nose with one more front still to come.

Rankin came up on deck at first light, bright eyed and cheery. He made the mistake of asking how things were going. Sandy voiced her objections to being out in the ocean in bad weather again, when we could be in the ICW. I chimed in with the exact same thought. To his credit, Rankin turned the boat right and headed to the Cape Fear River and the port of Southport, North Carolina. We had 35 nm to go, but the pounding was much less after the turn. The closer to shore we got, the less severe the wind became. Southport is a lovely little town, and we had a great visit.

Rankin hates the ICW, and I have learned to hate it as well, but we did the ditch to Florida with the exception of Georgia, which we did on the outside. Hannah met us in Titusville, Florida, three and a half weeks after we left Colington. We re-provisioned the boat, and the four of us sailed from Port Canaveral directly to Marsh Harbour, Abacos. We had a glorious sail on one tack and sailed for two nights and part of three days. At last, the journey was truly complete, we sailed to the Bahamas! Now, I just had to do it on MY boat.

By early summer of 2004, Hannah decided to go her separate way and moved out of my house. By September she had moved back to Richmond. I was without a partner in life and without a sailing partner. Another winter was to be spent in Colington. Yuck.

CHAPTER 48
NEW FIRST MATE

MY BEST AND CLOSEST FRIEND, Dave Enochs, suggested that I go on one of the online dating services to meet someone, and he suggested eHarmony.com. In November 2004 I signed up and began the involved process that is required to meet people on that service. Dave Enochs took photographs of me standing on the bow of *Southern Heat*, and I loaded them onto my eHarmony site.

I "talked" with a number of very nice women on the site, hoping to find someone who liked boats. One of the first I corresponded with was Camilla, a beautiful redhead from Arlington, Virginia. We "talked" on the dating site for several months, and then we both drove to Richmond, Virginia, to meet in person for the first time. The trip was about half way for both of us.

Camilla told the receptionist at the restaurant to come rescue her if she gave the "Hi" sign. I guess I did OK since I didn't get booted out of the joint. We both decided that another date would be appropriate, and we met again about a month later.

The truth be known, Camilla drove down to the Outer Banks to see if I really had a boat and, if so, what condition it was in. Smart woman. It turned out that Camilla spent some time on a very nice power boat, but was on a sailboat only once. OK, I guess I can train her, I thought.

The first visit to the Outer Banks netted zero time on *Southern Heat* as the weather was bad. She said, "This boat never leaves the dock." On the second visit to the Outer Banks, there was absolutely no wind. She said again, "This boat never leaves the dock." I replied, "OK, we will motor all over the Albemarle Sound, let's go."

Sure enough, once on the sound, there was no wind, so we motored. In a little while there were "cat's paws," slight ripples on the water, caused by the lightest of breezes. Soon there was enough breeze to raise the sails, which we did, and off we went for a very gentle sail. The wind built and built. Within a half-hour, we saw a sustained 30 knots of wind. All of my sails were deployed, and I really needed to reef. Camilla had no clue as to how to help. The boat, of course, was heeled to the gunnels and flying, albeit a bit out of control.

Camilla asked, "David, when does one get off the boat?" I lightly replied, "When we get back to the dock."

First I fell way off the wind and put *Southern Heat* on autopilot. With the jib blanketed by the main, I was easily able to furl in three quarters of the jib. Then I headed up into the wind and furled in half of the in mast furling mainsail. I bore off to close hauled, and *Southern Heat* was well balanced, tracking nicely, and under control. Ultimately, we had a fantastic sailing afternoon. That was Camilla's initiation to sailing.

Camilla was and is an international flight attendant, so adjusting to sailing was not difficult for her. She did, however, have trouble remembering from trip to trip what all of the lines were for. That is, until she discovered that sailboats can be raced. I had no idea of the competitive spirit that lived within her. Wow.

She decided that we needed to catch the neighbors' boat. "David, how do we catch them?" she asked competitively. "Remember the sail trim that I told you about? That is how you make the boat go fast," I replied. Camilla immediately perched herself on the cockpit side bulkhead and began trimming the jib. Soon, we picked up speed. It took awhile, but we caught the neighbors' boat. She was hooked!

After that event, Camilla took pride in trimming both the jib and the main. We have raced *Southern Heat* a few times, although she is very much a cruiser, and Camilla is always the jib trimmer. Male crew have instructions to not take her job from her; she can do it and is good at it. Someone might have to trim in the last inch if we are close hauled in strong wind, but other than that Camilla is self-sufficient.

CHAPTER 49
WE SAIL TO THE ABACOS

OUR ROMANTIC RELATIONSHIP became strong and stable, and I began talking to Camilla about sailing to the Bahamas for the winter. I really wanted to accomplish the feat of making it to the Bahamas on my own boat. Camilla was willing.

As we prepared for the trip, Camilla's flight-attendant experience showed. She was organized and understood that a cruising sailboat has only just so much stowage space available. We worked together to find all available space and use that space wisely. We made the trips to the "wholesale" big lot stores as well as the local grocery store to provision for the six-month live-aboard experience.

Camilla found fishnet bags that we filled with canned goods and then lowered into deep holds under the forward bed. Plastic bins were used in other places, and in some areas we stowed loose soft goods. Working as a team, we both had an idea of where various items were stowed.

I have found that cruisers tend to work right up to the last minute getting things ready for the trip. I did not want to be exhausted when it was time to leave the slip. Our departure date was November 1. A large storm moved up the East Coast and delayed our departure until the 4th. Thus, I got the rest I needed.

As we left Colington Harbour, I looked back to the east and the sun was just coming over the horizon. I retrieved the video camera and recorded the scene. That shot is still one of my favorites of all time. It was a glorious sunrise and the beginning of a new adventure and a wonderful relationship.

Everyone has his/her own philosophy of getting south. Camilla and I prefer to do as much ocean work as possible, within our own comfort zone of safety. On this, our first long trip, we motored all the way to Charleston, South Carolina, on the Intracoastal Waterway. A few cruisers write about making stops in various towns along the route, spending time in each location. My philosophy is to get south to warm weather as soon as possible. That thought is shared by the vast majority of cruisers, I think. Camilla agrees, although she really likes Charleston. If the weather is nice, move the boat, I say, as bad and cold weather is always chasing the south-bound cruiser.

Ultimately, once reaching Florida, it is prudent to make the hop across to the Abacos on the first available safe weather window. This is so because as winter closes in, the cold fronts become stronger and more frequent. Thus, always in the back of my mind is the thought to move the boat. That is not to say, that if we have to stop for a day or two for weather or another reason, I don't enjoy the area that we are visiting, not so. I enjoy it immensely. But with only eight hours of daylight in the winter months, we push hard when on the ICW.

We try to leave at first light and stop at about 1600 in the evening. We sail/motor anywhere from 50 to 70 plus nm a day. Thirty-mile trips are unheard of for us and we would think that we were wasting time if we stopped much before 1600. Sometimes you have to stop a little early or late as there is no place to stop at exactly 1600, for example.

The boat was tied up in Charleston for five days as Camilla had to fly to Chicago for flight attendant in-service training. I stayed with *Southern Heat* in Charleston. We had tied up at the Charleston Maritime Center, which was substantially less expensive than staying at any of the other marinas. The historical district was within walking/biking distance and a nice grocery store was two blocks away.

On her return date to the boat, Camilla expected to be in around 1600, too late to leave the dock. I was relaxing on the boat when I received a call on my cell phone from Camilla saying that she would be back by 1400. Wow, I had to move fast if we wanted to leave, and leaving would be a good idea as we had about a 36-hour weather window. We were going to sail on the outside from Charleston to the Saint Mary's River Inlet on the Georgia/Florida border, thus skipping the shallow waters and significant tides of the Georgia ICW.

The folding bikes were on the dock and needed to be stowed down below for sailing, the boat needed water, and I had to stow the shore-power cords. Better get to it and quickly. I was just finishing when Camilla walked down the dock.

We got out of the slip as quickly as possible, which is always a challenge at that marina due to the strong current, and headed into Charleston Harbor and toward the North Atlantic Ocean. This was to be Camilla's first ocean voyage on a sailboat. We motored out past Fort Sumter with a dolphin escort in dead calm conditions. The ocean was as flat as a pancake.

By then it was turning dark and Camilla went below to prepare something for supper. She grew very possessive of "her" galley and didn't particularly want me in there. She was efficient and particularly fast during cleanup. She learned quickly to be miserly with the fresh water.

After supper, Camilla went down for a nap since she was exhausted from her flying trip. At sometime around 0200, she came up to relieve me. Normally, we stand three-hour watches apiece, and I enforce that rule, particularly during night passages. This time had been an exception, and I had been on the helm for about 12 hours. This wasn't a big problem as weather conditions were calm, as was the ocean, which was still flat, and we had a full moon. I did need to get a little sleep for safety reasons, if nothing else.

Camilla got acclimated to the helm, and I went down for some sleep. We converted the dinette to a bed so that whoever was sleeping down below would be able to hear the on-watch crew if that person called for assistance. I had been asleep for a short while when I heard and smelled the engine (rubber burning) as well as heard, "David, something is wrong." "I know," I said. "I'm coming up."

The engine alarm had activated and was making a terrible noise. I shut down the engine, grabbed a flashlight, and opened one of the engine-access panels, knowing what to expect. Yep, I discovered a broken fan belt. I thought, "That is not too big a deal; I have spare belts and I know exactly what bolts to loosen to change out the belt."

We had anchored in a small creek just north of Charleston the evening before we went to Charleston and the following morning as we left the anchorage, the fan belt began to squeal. I had to drop anchor in the narrow ICW to tighten the belt. We made sécurité announcements on the marine VHF radio so that other boaters would know early on that we were stationary. Most boats slowed to almost dead stop as they crept by us. Two volunteered their spare belts. One, of course, blew by, rocking us crazily. The bottom line is that due to that experience, I did not have to investigate how to accomplish the immediate task and I had the new belt installed and we were underway again within a half-hour. I went back to bed.

The moon finally disappeared around 0400. When I came back on deck, Camilla observed that "This ocean sailing is nothing like I thought it would be; it's easy." I quickly advised her that this was very much the exception to the rule.

That afternoon, we motored into St. Mary's Inlet and eight miles up the St. Mary's River to the water town of St. Mary, where we anchored for several days. We arrived on Thanksgiving eve and had heard that the town of St. Mary hosted a Thanksgiving meal for cruisers each Thanksgiving. We decided to attend.

Thanksgiving morning was stormy and raining. Would we dinghy into town for the big get together? We had not decided. Finally, it stopped raining and the wind lessened, so we headed into town with our covered-dish offering. The local hotel had opened its bottom floor for the function, and approximately three hundred cruisers were in attendance.

Disappointingly, we found most people to be engaged in their own conversations and they seemed to be a little cliquish. With the experience we now have, that might not seem to be the case. At any rate, we met a couple, Rick and Linda on S/V *Sojourner*, who were very nice.

A couple of days later as we pulled out of an anchorage early in the morning, a sailboat motored by and yelled to us, "Hey, *Southern Heat*, we took your picture and will give them to you when we see you in the Abacos." When Rick and Linda actually did meet us in the Abacos, Linda told the story of the photo session and said that I had a look on my face that said, "Yeah right, I'm sure that we will really see you in the Abacos." She continues to like telling that story, and she was right, that is exactly what I was thinking.

While we do tend to make the "wild dash south," the ICW does have its unique beauty. North Carolina and South Carolina possess miles and miles of serene beauty in the form of marshes and flowing savannahs. At times the waterway is narrow and winding, and at other times the boat is on open bodies of wide water. Florida offers white sandy shores, clear blue water, seabirds, and numerous dolphins. In some places the waterway is comprised of manmade canals, some dating back to colonial times, such as Virginia's and North Carolina's Dismal Swamp Canal, surveyed by George Washington.

Sunsets along the ICW can be stunning. Imagine being anchored in a quiet creek without a sound but a few water birds looking for their supper. As the sun sets, the sky turns various shades of red, pink, and purple. In one such instance, I retrieved both the video and still cameras. I photographed the outrageous colors of the skyline as the sun plunged toward earth. Thinking I was done, I put the cameras away, only to find that the sky had changed dramatically in the short time that I was down below. Back to the cameras for more photography. Every minute or so, the picture changed again.

As we moved farther south along Florida's east coast on the ICW, we looked for a place to stop for the night. The cruising guide recommended a small anchorage about 20 nm north of St. Augustine. The guide mentioned current running in the creek and said to stay 100 feet off the red channel marker at the creek's entrance, but not to get too close to the south shore as it shoals out a ways. Hmmm, sounded interesting, or is that challenging?

We arrived a little later than I preferred, and the anchorage was crowded with cruising boats. We inched our way into the mouth of the creek and got beyond the channel marker. I moved forward into the creek as far as I could without encroaching on other boats, and Camilla dropped the hook (anchor). After setting the anchor, I settled into the cockpit with a cold beer to relax for a bit after a long day of motoring on the ICW.

Just before sunset another boat pulled in. *Where is he going?* I thought. *There is no room.* The captain made it just past the channel marker and dropped his anchor. He disappeared down below and a few minutes later re-appeared on deck with a set of bagpipes. The piper moved to the foredeck, where he began to play the pipes. That man was good! I expected him to play one song and stop, but, no, he continued to play and I was very glad that he did. What a way to end the day.

Southern Heat continued her trek south, down the ICW to Fort Pierce, Florida. By then, I'd had my fill of the ICW and wanted no more of it. The last leg to Fort Pierce was plagued with strong crosswinds for the entire day. The channel was narrow, creating tension for the captain who had to constantly work at keeping the boat in the channel and not blown to the side.

Looking at the charts, North Palm Beach and Lake Worth appeared to be a day sail away on the outside. I talked with the professional captain in the adjacent slip in the marina and he said, "Go out the inlet and turn right, that is all there is to it."

"How far offshore should I go?" I asked.

"You don't have to," he said. "Just get beyond the breakers and you will be fine." Man, that sounded fantastic to me. I studied my paper charts and the electronic charts to make final preparations for the following morning, and it looked easy. Camilla and I walked around town that evening and found an Italian restaurant that offered a great meal.

We left a little after first light and found the wind to be light. We had a very relaxed motor-sail to West Palm Beach. After entering the Class A inlet, we turned north and wound our way up to the north end of Lake Worth to a very protected anchorage, outlined by exclusive Florida homes with numerous palm trees and a couple of marinas.

Dave Graf and Doug Bendura, Doug being another great sailing buddy, were to drive down from Virginia to meet us at West Palm Beach on Saturday evening and make the crossing with us to the Abacos. Saturday morning *Southern Heat* moved to a marina farther south in Lake Worth to meet Dave and Doug. When we pulled into the slip Doug and Dave were there on the dock waiting for us; beside them on the dock were two very heavy 4D deep cycle 12 volt house batteries that I had asked them to bring.

After a quick beer, Dave, Doug, and I removed the old batteries and replaced them with the new. The four of us then drove Doug's vehicle to the local West Marine, where we purchased a few last-minute items and a new shore-power inlet receptacle. Upon returning to the boat, Doug and Dave removed the damaged receptacle and installed the new one.

Later, we drove to a nice restaurant district for an early supper. Returning to the boat, we all took a nap, as we were to leave the slip before 0300 to begin the voyage to the Abacos. It was difficult to fall asleep due to the excitement in the air; shortly, we would be headed on the last leg of the trip. We did manage to get a nap before the alarm clock awoke us for our 0245 departure. Just off the marina was a bridge that opened on the hour, which we needed to intercept at 0300.

It was good to have the old team of Dave Graf and Dave Hope back together again. I had Dave Graf go forward with a spotlight and a family frequency radio head set, to look for channel markers and obstructions. Oh, and he was to help me stay in the channel. We had to motor several miles in the ICW and then turn right to enter the channel to the ocean inlet. Dave did an admirable job on the bow, looking for markers and other things that we did not want to hit.

Ultimately, we found the inlet and headed out into the ocean swell. As we moved away from the inlet, the moderate swell decreased and we were seeing an easy passage. The trip from West Palm Beach to West End, Grand Bahama, was 56 nm. I wanted to arrive with the sun still high in the air, thus the 3 AM departure. The wind remained at 10 knots, on our stern, and we motor-sailed.

At sometime around 1300, we began to see structure on the eastern horizon – we were approaching the Bahamas! The excitement in the cockpit kicked up a notch. A short while later, Doug, who was sitting in the cockpit facing aft, leaning against the coach roof bulkhead, pointed out behind the boat and said in an excited voice, "What is that?!"

At first glance it looked like a huge log about 75 yards directly behind us and perpendicular to us; that is, until it spouted. "It's a whale!" we all shouted in unison. That was a close encounter; we didn't miss him by much.

As we approached West End, Dave Graf went forward with the binoculars to pick out the entrance to the little harbor. It looked as though we were going to sail right into the wall. Closing with the structure, it became apparent where the channel lay. It was so exciting to be pulling into Bahamian waters on my own boat, finally. All of us were to the point of giddiness with excitement and fatigue, as no one had slept more than a catnap since leaving Lake Worth.

After doing the extensive immigration paperwork and paying the $300 boat fee, I felt like I had arrived. We had three more daytrips to finally arrive at Marsh Harbour, Abaco, our final destination. Dave Graf's cycle wasn't complete yet, but it would be upon reaching Marsh Harbor.

Before relaxing too much, I discussed with the dockmaster the two available routes toward Marsh Harbour, the shorter route and the safe, longer route. For several miles, the shorter route had 5 ½ to 6 feet of depth in the nearly unmarked channel. The safe route carried plenty of water, but was miles out of the way. The dockmaster, who grew up navigating the short route, recommended it. I decided against the short route, thinking his familiarity with the route might get me into trouble.

Once again, a little after first light, we were underway. Dave Graf lobbied for sailing, but the wind was still 10 knots on our stern, so we again motor-sailed. We crossed from the deep blue of the Atlantic Ocean into the beautiful light-blue/green waters of the Little Bahama Banks where depths ranged from 7 to 20 feet. I was accustomed to those depths after sailing on the Albemarle Sound, "No problem, mon."

We had a leisurely and relaxed motor-sail and arrived at Great Sale Cay at 1600. Great Sale is a horseshoe-shaped cay out in the middle of nowhere, but it has great protection except from the west. It is a favorite anchorage for cruisers headed to and from the Abacos. A few beers and a great meal on the grill supplemented by Camilla's side dishes finished off a wonderful day.

We had two more days to Marsh harbor, and I couldn't wait. As we proceeded toward and then down the Sea of Abaco, the forecast for the evening grew more and more ominous. We were to get high wind from the northwest. That would leave the anchorages along our route unprotected from the wind. I chose to go to Spanish Cay marina for the night. Mid-afternoon we pulled into Spanish Cay and after taking on some diesel fuel, we took our assigned slip. What I didn't know was that a hurricane a couple of years prior had compromised the rock bulkhead protecting the marina. A good portion of the waves from the northwest wind would pound right through the damaged areas.

The French Canadian lady who was managing the marina turned out to be the chef for the evening. We each chose our entrée and submitted it to her before 1700. She acquired the fish and prepared our meals at our designated reservation time. The meals were excellent, but set a bar that would not be matched by any other restaurant we visited during our five months in the Abacos. Not only did the marina manager prepare fantastic meals for us, but she told us that a number of the marinas in Marsh Harbour had special rates for seasonal patrons. She graciously offered her telephone in the morning so that we could call the various marinas to ascertain information on rates.

Sleeping the last night before arriving at Marsh Harbour was difficult at best. The waves did, in fact, pound through the damaged breakwater and slam into *Southern Heat* most of the night. We were rocked and bounced but safe. The morning brought light to moderate wind and seas, and we were ready for the last day hop to Marsh Harbour.

After passing Green Turtle Cay to our port, *Southern Heat* would have to negotiate notorious Whale Pass to once again enter the Atlantic Ocean in order to navigate to the south end of Whale Cay and re-enter the Sea of Abaco. The Whale, as it is called, can be extremely dangerous when in a "rage," with huge waves forcing themselves through the relatively narrow coral outcropping ocean pass. It is always prudent to get a report on the conditions at The Whale before committing one's boat to the pass.

We had been too far north to receive the cruisers' net report of The Whale conditions for that morning. Doug found a potential source of information in the cruisers' guide of the Abacos and called on his worldwide cell phone. The gentleman answered and said that The Whale was "very doable" that morning. I had been through The Whale several years ago on *Heart of Texas* with Rankin and Sandy and had a vague idea of how to go about it. We found gentle ocean swells as we popped out of the pass and into the ocean.

Re-entering the Sea of Abaco at the south end of Whale Cay, we began looking for the remnants of the cruise line channel markers, which would lead us between Spoil Cay and the north end of Great Guana Cay. Dave Graf was at the helm and having a great time. We worked our way down the channel and saw Marsh Harbour up in the distance.

I told Dave to head toward the tall radio tower in the distance, which he did. In a short while we were approaching the harbor of Marsh Harbour itself. After several telephone calls and a discussion between ourselves, we decided to take a slip at Harbor View Marina, which turned out to be an excellent choice and is now our marina of choice. All of the Marsh Harbour marinas are in shallow 6 feet water, but all *Southern Heat* needs is 5 feet, and I was accustomed to shallow water anyway.

The dock hands led us to our assigned slip and assisted with our lines. Once secured, it began to dawn on me that we were actually there. I had finally made it, on my own boat. I was grinning from ear to ear. I was standing on the aft deck when a dinghy passed by with a man and woman aboard. I waved and they yelled up to me, "Did you just get here?" With a big smile I replied, "Yes, we just tied up a few minutes ago and I am really excited to be here!" Ed and Valerie were anchored out in the harbor and turned out to be really great friends as time passed on.

As the sun was getting low in the western sky, Dave, Doug, and I walked out to the end of the dock as far out as we could get, each with a cold beer, and watched the sun set. From then on I thought of that special moment each time that I walked out there.

Dave Graf had finally "completed" the trip from hell, and I had finally brought my own boat to the Bahamas and was living a new life. Jeff Akins and another cousin, Bruce Akins, would fly to Marsh Harbour later that season to sail on *Southern Heat*, thus completing Jeff's trip from hell.

Hannah had gone her separate way, but previously had flown to Marsh Harbour with me when we accepted the invitation from *Heart of Texas* to visit shortly after the loss of *Summer Heat*. Further, she had met us in Titusville when I sailed with *Heart of Texas* and we all made the crossing to the Abacos in 2003.

Jammer was the only crew of the ill-fated *Summer Heat* to not finish the trip, but he did finish his own voyage and I know he was chewing on something fun and looking down on us that very special evening.

The voyage of *Summer Heat* is complete.

Captain David P. Hope
S/V *Summer Heat*, r.i.p.

ABOUT THE AUTHOR

DAVID PHILIP HOPE served as a first lieutenant in the U.S. Army during the Viet Nam War era after graduating from Infantry Officer Candidates' School, Fort Benning GA. He completed his undergraduate degree from East Carolina University with a B.S.P. in Criminal Justice. He then served as a police officer in the Chesterfield County Police Department, Chesterfield County, VA from 1976 until his retirement in 2002. He rose to the rank of police major and ultimately had 250 police officers, supervisors, and managers in his command.

The author lives on the Outer Banks of North Carolina with his fiancée and his English springer spaniel. From there he sails the waters of Chesapeake Bay, the Albemarle and Pamlico Sounds, and south to Florida and the Bahamas. He has said many times that he is happiest when on his boat.

Additional information and pictures can be found at www.facebook.com/SummerHeatthebook.

ALSO AVAILABLE
FROM RAMBLING STAR PUBLISHING

Around the World in 80 Years: The Oldest Man to Sail Alone around the World - Twice!
By Harry L. Heckel, Jr. with Florence Heckel Russell

At the advanced ages of 78 and 89, Harry L. Heckel, Jr., fulfilled a dream: he sailed alone around the world, not once, but twice! This Old Man of the Sea goes global, describing with a dry wit and a keen eye, the 54 countries and islands he visited, plus the sail to get there. Armchair travelers and sailors alike will be enthralled by the adventures of this Ancient Mariner: from the Killing Fields of Cambodia to the Great Wall of China, from avoiding pirates off Somalia to almost capsizing off Madagascar.

An inspiring tale that proves that age is no deterrent to fulfilling your dream!

Heading South: Tales from the RV Trail
By Florence Heckel Russell

To escape Cleveland's winter, former reporter Florence Heckel Russell and her husband head South in their new RV. When they return after spending months together in a 23-by-8 foot space, they are, miraculously, still married.

From Mammoth Cave to Carlsbad Caverns, the couple adjusts to close-quarter living as they stumble through adventures: fun, frustrating and at times downright scary.

Made in the USA
San Bernardino, CA
04 August 2014